Living the

DEciSioN

A pocket guide to cramming 72 years into 27

Authored by

Phillip Bennett

Continued by

Jaime Richards

ISBN: 1479344923

ISBN-13: 9781479344925

Library of Congress Control Number: 2012917677

CreateSpace Independent Publishing Platform

North Charleston, South Carolina

An Unplanned Introduction from Phil's Co-author

I met Phillip Bennett in September of 1998 when he sort of swayed into my eighth-grade U.S. History classroom. I didn't know he had Friedreich's ataxia (FA). I didn't know what Friedreich's ataxia was. I was curious about his awkward gait, but only for a moment. Quickly, I forgot about it because Phillip fit right into that class. He smiled, joked, and, like most every other thirteen-year-old, showed little interest in the United States Constitution.

As the school year wore on, I learned more about both Phillip and FA. That February, I traveled with a group of fifty students, including Phillip, to Washington, DC, for the weeklong Washington Workshops program. His mom, Valerie, joined us as one of our chaperones. While we were there, she and Phil would attend an important FA convention that was being held that same week in D.C.

After Phil moved on to high school, I didn't see him much. We'd cross paths at a track meet or some other high school or community function. Occasionally, I'd run into Valerie at the grocery store and get a "Phil update."

Not long after Phil graduated from San Jose State, I saw Val near a checkout counter at Safeway. She told me he was on Facebook and that I should friend him. I did. A few months later Phil posted the saddest, most depressing Facebook status I've ever seen:

"What the fuck did I ever do to deserve this life?"

It was so unlike him. Phil's mood was usually light and upbeat. So I messaged him and said I had a plan. I suggested that we meet. When we did, I told him that the world needed him to write his story. I knew he had done all kinds of crazy, interesting stuff. I knew that he was fascinating and charming. To know Phil was to love Phil.

I also knew that he had been through hell and had overcome mountainous obstacles. His story, I was sure, would be motivating. If Phil could go through life with a smile on his face, we all can. At least we could cut back on our whining. Additionally, I knew Phillip could write. In junior high he was way better than his peers. In college, he was a journalism major.

So we began.

We'd meet in person or on Skype, or Phil would e-mail me what he wrote. FA was robbing him of his keyboarding skills, so sometimes he dictated to Valerie. Then she would write his words and send them on to me.

A few months into the project, I joked with Phil, "You better not die before we finish this book!" He laughed and then got back to business, sharing another story from his heartbreaking yet uplifting life.

Truth is, even though Philip was cursed with Friedreich's ataxia, none of us who knew him expected him to die any time soon. When, at twenty-five, he began writing *Living the Decision*, he had already lived longer than many doctors believed he would. Yet, because there have been people with FA who have lived to be as old as forty, we expected Phil to live at least that long.

When he didn't, it shocked us. It shouldn't have, but it did. When I learned of Phil's untimely death, before the sadness engulfed me, my first thought was, *Phil, I told you not to die! How are we going to finish your book now?!* Truthfully, though, there wasn't any question about it. Somehow, we'd finish the book. Phil had given me plenty of material. Even though he wouldn't be physically here to tell me precisely how to organize it, I'd been working with him long enough to feel confident about how he'd want the book to look. More important, Phil, in his words, would be "pissed as hell" if we didn't finish and publish *Living the Decision*.

—Jaime Richards

ᴛᴇɴɢᴡᴀʀ ᴛᴇxᴛ

P r o l o g u e

ᴛᴇɴɢᴡᴀʀ ᴛᴇxᴛ

**"All we have to decide is what to do
with the time that is given to us."**

—Gandalf in *The Fellowship of the Ring*

When I was sixteen, I had my friendly neighborhood tattoo artist ink Gandalf's wise words in the Elvish Tengwar font, wrapping them around my left bicep. My tattoo represents more than simply some bizarre and agonizing fetish; it carries truth for us all, but it is especially meaningful and relevant to me.

I am the unlucky owner of a charming affliction called Friedreich's ataxia (FA), an inherited, progressive genetic neuromuscular disorder. It has damaged my sensory and motor nerves, making it difficult for me to balance, walk, or speak coherently. I'm stuck in a wheelchair.

I'm a journalist, not a historian, but here are the facts: Nikolaus Friedreich was a nineteenth-century German neurologist. In 1863, he was the first to diagnose what I have. Ataxia is the inability to coordinate muscle movements. Even when I could still walk, I did so clumsily. FA is rare. Only about one in fifty thousand Americans get it. So I guess that makes me special.

Although I was born with FA, its symptoms didn't show up right away. I was a typical little kid. I rode my bike and played soccer—my golden years, so to speak. It wasn't until I was ten that the doctors told me that my life would never be normal. Gradually, as FA continued to pick off my nerve cells, my condition would deteriorate until I died. There is no cure.

As I learned in my high school biology class, my life expectancy is between thirty and forty years. I write this at twenty-five, so I write this book with a sense of urgency. Sure, any one of us could die tomorrow while trying to cross the street, but my days are probably more numbered than yours. What I decide to do with the time given to me is a constant concern.

One of the ways I've chosen to spend my precious time is writing this book. I'm writing it for four reasons:

1. To raise awareness. Hardly anyone has even heard of Friedreich's Ataxia. I want to change this. It's sadly comical how few people, even doctors, understand what Friedreich's Ataxia is.

2. Instead of passively letting Friedreich's Ataxia chip away at the remainder of my life, I've decided to take charge of it. Instead of waiting for other people's efforts to lead to a cure, I've decided to make the cure happen sooner. One way for me to do this is use this book's proceeds to fund FA research.

3. Perspective. We all have our struggles. I'm not saying that mine are more difficult than yours. But I can offer you a unique perspective on how to cope with life's daily difficulties. Further, I'm qualified to close the void between the textbook definition of FA and what it's actually like to live with it.

4. Inspiration. Despite my crappy condition, I'm proud of my positive attitude. It's one of the reasons I was chosen as a Muscular Dystrophy Association Goodwill Ambassador. I do everything I can to live well, and I hope to encourage you to do the same.

No doubt, Friedreich's ataxia sucks. It has ruined my life. Not many days go by when I don't ask myself, "Why me? What did I ever do to deserve this?" So far, I haven't been able to figure it out. Still, it's not all bad. I have good days. I haven't lost my sense of humor. I've had some wild experiences—on both ends of the spectrum.

So, maybe my purpose is to share my stories and what I've learned about living, hoping that they might make others' lives a little more meaningful and a little bit better.

In November 2011, my parents and I were at BORP—the Bay Area Outreach and Recreation Program—checking out trikes. (BORP is a San Francisco Bay Area provider and promoter of accessible sports and recreation vehicles and gear for guys like me.) Among the other customers there that day was a beautiful young woman who zipped around the place in a sleek, sporty wheelchair.

I was too gutless to roll over and hit on her, yet I couldn't help gawking at her. Before my jaw dropped all the way to the ground, I turned away, but I still managed to eavesdrop on her conversation. Apparently, she was (and probably still is) competing nationally in wheelchair sports.

I admired her. Not only was she a total hottie, but she has obviously made the most of what life has thrown at her, using her strengths to inspire others.

As much as I would love to state otherwise, the physical exertion required to excel in wheelchair sporting events is not one of my strengths. Alas, I have a shirt in my closet that depicts me as a "pale scrawny guy." Seeing her got me thinking of ways in which I could impact the world. My skills and strengths have nothing to do with wheelchair athletics. I am not a jock. I am a journalist.

Not long ago, I met Kyle Bryant, a guy about my age who, too, has been cursed with Friedreich's ataxia. In just three years, by organizing and leading bike rides across the country, he has been able to raise more than seven hundred thousand dollars! Somewhat ashamedly, I admit that I'm a tinge jealous of Kyle. He has already accomplished so much for the cause.

What can I do? I refuse to wait around for someone else to find the cure that will save my life. Sure, by organizing fund-raiser dinner parties, my mother and I managed to yank two hundred thousand dollars in donations for FA research, but I'm not satisfied. While I was gawking at that gorgeous girl, I accepted the reality that wheelchair athletics are her forte, but they aren't mine. Biking is Kyle's, but it's not mine.

What is mine?

How am I going to leave *my* thumbprint on the world? One way I *won't* do it is lounging around the house or glued to my computer screen playing World of Warcraft.

During the time that I was a journalism major at San Jose State, several of my professors urged me to write a book about my life. I was too busy with school then, but I did think it was a cool idea, and it would fulfill one of my primary goals: to be remembered. I want to be remembered as the guy who shattered the damnation that plagues my life and the lives of so many others with FA—my brothers and sisters who trek along this same worn-out brick road that I'm on, most behind me, but a few further along this path into deterioration.

Until now, I have not ventured into the world of fund-raising without the shelter of my mommy. But now, with school behind me, I have the time to focus on what I do best—write.

As far as I know, there has never been a book written by someone with Friedreich's ataxia, and I will not pretend to write an autobiography that accurately depicts everybody at every variable stage of this dreadful disease. I can, however, share my experiences and tell you what I've learned about living with FA and what I've learned about life.

Additionally, *Living the Decision* will include takes from my mom, dad, and a few others who know me well. It's important, I believe, to hear their perspective. How has what I have affected *them?* Straight up, in their own words, they'll tell you.

I have friends who are in the latter stages of FA. They can't work a keyboard anymore. Before I reach that point, I want—no, I *need*—to get this done. It's what I've decided to do with the time that has been given to me.

Note: I don't want this to be all about me. So, throughout the book, family members and friends will be sharing their thoughts and memories. When they do, their passages are written in *italics*.

þλ ˈᴄᴊᴏᴊᴘᴍ́ ᴄᴏ̆ϒɭ
The Golden Years

My journalism professors warned against beginning my story with "I was born…" or any other rudimentary cliché, but I've always enjoyed devouring the forbidden fruit. So…

I was born on July 8, 1984, in Hayward, California. Of course, I don't remember much about that day or my early years. But my mom sure does.

Mom: *There is something very special about my son. I realize that thought has been expressed by every parent since the dawn of time. But really, seriously, MY son is very special. I don't mean just that he is brilliant, which he is. Or that he is handsome, which he most certainly is. Or that he lights up a room when he smiles, which he does. Since he was born, my son has had an ethereal, otherworldly quality about him.*

The being born part was just funny. Phillip decided to come into this world a month ahead of schedule, and just to make sure no one got bored in the process, he wasn't going to come in smoothly. Those who understand what goes on when a baby is born will empathize with my concern when the doctor informed us that our baby was breech. Immediately after the cesarean delivery, my doctors announced that I had a baby girl. One of the staff even wrote "girl" on all three hospital bracelets. It was only when they finally managed to untangle Phillip's legs from the incredibly uncomfortable position he was in before birth that someone discovered he was actually a boy. Girl was quickly crossed out on the three bracelets, and boy was written in its place. I still have two of those bracelets.

So does my dad.

Dad: *When Phillip was just a lump in his mom's belly, I gave him his first nickname: Blasto, named after the early state of cell growth, blastocyst.*

His mother and I had just started a six-week Lamaze class to get ready for him, but, being an impatient little bugger, he decided to put his foot through the sack just two weeks into the Lamaze session.

We zipped over to Kaiser Hospital in Hayward where we were warned the birth would be a breach presentation, followed by a C-section. When they pulled Phillip out, a nurse announced, "You have a baby girl!" I had time to congratulate Valerie on her "Ashley Rose" before the doctor spotted a huge pair of balls and promptly declared that our baby was definitely not a girl. After that, I called him Big Balls Bennett. I rushed home and repainted his bedroom blue.

Sharon Cooper, one of my mom's closest friends, knew me—or at least of me—before I was born.

Sharon: *I suspected that Phillip was on the way when Valerie refused wine, coffee, and dessert at a good restaurant. Phillip was about the most perfect baby anyone could want. He was healthy, cute, affectionate, obedient, and quiet. Long before he could talk, he would do things when asked. If Valerie needed her purse, he could go into the next room and get it. It was clear that he understood language long before he spoke.*

I'm not sure when I first thought he should be talking, but wasn't. He could say "Mama," "Dada," and "no" (with a stamp of his cute, little foot), but nothing that you could call real speech. There were several frustrating times when Phillip would point, grunt, and sigh, but I couldn't figure out what he wanted.

One day, my husband, James, and I arrived for dinner and Phillip answered the door and greeted us. "Hi, James and Sharon," he announced. "We're having strawberry short-cake for dessert!"

He spoke as clearly as many adults. I don't believe I ever heard him use baby talk or even make a grammatical error. Not long after Phillip first spoke, he was playing chess on the computer. He only came up to my waist, but he still beat me! I tried to blame it on the wine, but he didn't believe that for a minute.

According to Mom, when I was just a tyke, I was quite the ham. Perhaps if my fortune had been fortunate, I could have been a movie star or something cool like that.

Mom: *You might think that Phillip's atypical entrance into this world foretold that he would become a difficult or contrary child, but the exact opposite turned out to be the case. He smiled constantly. We have albums and albums of photographs, and in every one of them Phillip, without fail, is beaming at the camera. He never went through the terrible twos. He enjoyed the company of people, and everyone adored him. Total strangers would approach us in airports and restaurants just to be close to Phillip. It was as if he had an aura about him that people wanted to share. He was his grandfather's fourth grandchild, and second grandson, but the first with whom he bonded. Friends who equate children* with elephants—they like both, but wouldn't want to live with either—were struck by something magical they saw in Phillip and connected with him.

One of my favorite photos was taken in Hawaii. Phillip and his dad went deep-sea fishing. His brother, Brian, and I stayed on land, because neither of our stomachs could find any pleasure in such an excursion. The sea was particularly rough that day, so the other patrons, and even Phillip's dad, were feeling the effects of seasickness. No one was catching anything either, so you might have thought that Phillip would have gotten bored. On the contrary. The picture shows him wearing sunglasses and a flap hat, a can of Coke in one hand, his Where's Waldo? book in the other and a bag of cheese twists at his side. While the rest of the passengers were turning green, Phillip was pouring over his book, while downing a Coke and cheese twists.

Dad's memories of my early years were also generally positive.

Dad: Phillip loved pacifiers and needed at least two at any one time. Sometimes he'd hold one in each hand and one in his mouth. We eventually broke him of the habit. I took him to Toys"R"Us and told him that he could buy anything in the store with his pacifiers. He bought a Lego set.

My son was a beautiful baby. Because he didn't have to battle his way through the birth canal, he wasn't beaten up. On the other hand, he was the world's worst sleeper. At most, *he'd sleep a two-hour stretch. He almost drove his parents insane!*

Phillip was a bright, well-behaved young child—a joy to be around. He was a Lego grandmaster. He could simply look at the massive pirate ship depicted on the Lego box and then assemble it in only a few nonstop hours. At school, he did well academically, but he wasn't much into sports. He loved Nintendo, especially the games that required thinking through challenges. The only shoot-'em-up game he liked was James Bond. Phillip spent hours playing the Legend of Zelda, and we got quite used to hearing the Zelda theme.

Although my passion for video games has waned with age, my love of food hasn't. I've always savored my meals. I especially enjoy pizza and pasta. Italian restaurants are one of life's great pleasures. From early on, my appetite and even-tempered demeanor impressed my mom.

Mom: *Phillip came everywhere with us. He flew twelve times before his first birthday, including trips to Canada and Hawaii. He could adapt to new environments, new people, and new foods without stress or fuss. Before his second birthday, he traveled with us to Florida and England, where he spent two weeks coping with and adjusting to jet lag, new environments, and strange people. Before his third birthday, we traveled to Mexico, where he slipped in the slick tiled shower and split open the back of his head. Thirty minutes after his* *sutures, acting as if nothing unusual had happened, there was Phillip, inhaling his dinner, amazing his fellow diners, including his parents, who were shakily bringing a glass of wine to their lips.*

Phillip loved to eat. And eat. And eat! From birth to today, I've never had to worry about his nutrition. He has always had a wonderful appetite. When he was a baby, just learning to eat food from a spoon, he gave a very good impression of a baby bird. At the sight of anything edible, his mouth would fly open in anticipation and wouldn't close until the spoon crossed his lips. When Phillip was still eating in a high chair, we took him out to dinner at the Old Spaghetti Factory in San Jose. We ordered him a plate of spaghetti that was about the same size he was. While he devoured it, people from surrounding tables watched, first with interest, then with amusement, and finally with amazement. An elderly gentleman came over and commented, "If I hadn't seen it with my own eyes, I would have never believed he could eat all that!"

Phillip also inherited my stomach for tolerating blood and gore and his father's stomach for being impervious to motion sickness. The result? Absolutely nothing makes him sick! When he was four, his dad, Tim, seriously injured his thumb. We had to drag Phillip with us to the emergency room...

I clearly remember that. My father was a sign manufacturer. He was constantly hurting himself. Even though that was expected in his line of work, he took it to an unexpected new level. Once, just before lunch, he drilled a big black hole into his thumb.

Urgently, my mom stuffed me into the car along with my bloody father and drove like a lunatic to the hospital. After filling out the admission paperwork, we were led into a room where we had to wait. And wait. And wait! Not having eaten lunch, I was starving. So my mom bought me my favorite snack—cheese balls.

I took them into the examining room where a doctor was working on my dad's open wound. While my dad grew more and more queasy, I was unaffected. I was enjoying my cheese balls. Always willing to share, I leaned forward and offered one to Dad. He declined, but his doctor turned around and said, "I'll take one." I spent the next few minutes casually shoveling cheese balls into his mouth.

I guess it's good that I have a strong stomach. Hospitals and medical procedures have never bothered me.

For whatever reason, from a freakishly early age, I've been virtually fearless. When I was still a preschooler, my dad sent me down into the crawl space beneath our house to help him run some wiring. Because I was little, I could crawl around down there much more easily than Dad. Maybe because I had not seen any of the *Arachnophobia* movies, I wasn't afraid. I got dressed in my Spider-Man pajamas, slipped through a space in our floor, and got the job done. When I emerged from the depths, I was covered from head to foot in cobwebs.

By the time I was eight, I had learned that the easiest way for me to get an adrenaline rush was by climbing the thirty-foot maple tree that stood right outside my bedroom window. Like a little monkey, I would scale up to where the branches could barely hold me. Maybe that's when and where I developed my fascination for heights. I remember going over to friends' houses and enjoying climbing to the tops of all the trees in their backyards.

When I was in first grade, I could still run—almost like the other kids—and I was quite proud of my performance in the school Wildcat Fun Run. Here I am showing off the lap marks on my arm. Looking back I wonder if it predicted my future love of tattoos.

Like practically every kid who grows up in California, I played on a youth soccer team. My dad was one of our coaches.

Dad: *We signed him up for soccer. I was the assistant coach. Phillip did not run like other kids. It was a flailing type of running. Still, for a while, he enjoyed playing. It irritated me when Moni, the head coach, kept him on the sidelines a lot. Truth was, the game was always a struggle for him. Eventually he lost interest and stopped playing.*

Even so, thanks to soccer, I met Dane Lentz. We ended up going to elementary, junior high, and high school together. On our high school track team, we both threw the shot put and discus. Then Dane followed me to Chabot Junior College and, later, to San Jose State where we both majored in journalism. I can't lose the guy! But I wouldn't want to. We became lifelong friends.

Here's what Dane remembers about us being soccer teammates:

Dane: *After meeting Phil in third or fourth grade on that club soccer team, I knew something was different about him. He stumbled around a lot. I remember one game where I was playing goalie and Phil was running down the field toward the other end…putting it bluntly, he looked like a newborn baby deer trying to walk. I wasn't raised to say anything negative about anyone, and I wasn't going to start with Phil.*

When I was nine, I started karate. A friend's father was an instructor. At that point, I was still on my feet. But I wasn't all that steady. So I took up karate to improve my balance and coordination and to keep physically active. (I was never much into physical activity. I preferred reading books or building Lego sets.) Yet, I enjoyed karate and tried hard. At the end of my second year, I was named Student of the Year. I was awarded a big trophy, which still sits on my chest of drawers.

I also learned to ride a bike. I don't remember feeling as if it was especially difficult for me—it took me a few tries before I made it down the driveway, but that is to be expected. Dad, however, saw it differently.

Dad: *Phillip learned to ride a bike, but he became reluctant to pedal to the store with his brother and me. I would berate him for spending too much time playing Nintendo and not enough time playing outside. When he did ride with us, his handlebars shook. There were other hints that all was not well. By the time he was nine, Phillip was becoming progressively clumsier. He would sometimes slip on our hardwood floors and spill his cereal.*

Girls liked me! In elementary school, an especially cute one named Holly Davis remembers how she spent many of her recesses.

Holly: *I chased Phillip around the blacktop because he was cute. Adorable actually. I told him once, "Your light shines through brighter than anyone I know." I felt that even then.*

One of the best weeks of my life was when I got to cut first grade for a week and visit Hawaii's Big Island. That's where I had one of my greatest adventures—the day we checked out the erupting volcano, Kilauea. I even remember clearly what I wore on my feet: little white, girly sandals.

Although the whole family went to watch the lava flows, my mom and I were the two adventurous spirits who made it to where we could safely see where the lava flowed through the ground, under our feet, on its way to the ocean. There was a hell of a lot of steam, so my mom told me to stay fifty feet back while she ventured forward and took a few pictures from right at the edge.

I was left there, gazing at the crazy idiots who were milling around near the spot where the lava was entering the ocean, creating a gigantic steam vent. The clouds looked threatening. Splatters of magma flew through the air, landing near the foolhardy mob, which included my mother.

Back then, I was fascinated by lava and volcanoes. So I was compelled to venture out to see the real thing, even if there was an endless river of boiling magma right beneath our feet! When I finally got close, I was disappointed *not* to be one of those maniacs dodging falling deposits of burning hot magma, yet I understood why my mom ordered me to keep a safe distance.

Gingerly traipsing over the lava-blanketed road, we made it to our car where my dad and brother, safely nestled inside it, had been waiting for us. I took off my sandals and socks and examined my feet. It turns out the magma was not the only hazard I should have worried about. After peeling off my toeless sandals, it was obvious that they had only partially protected my feet from the brutal environment. The little shards of glass that had formed on the surface of the lava had made themselves tiny homes in the spaces between my toes, which were leaking blood.

Later, I did get to see the red-hot magma up close, but from the security of a helicopter. I have a vivid memory of lava oozing, then cascading down the inside of the enormous crater. It was so hot in that little metal capsule that the soles of my shoes nearly melted onto the helicopter floor.

When I returned to school, as a memento—and to prove I was there—I gave little lava rocks to my classmates.

My mom and dad's take on how the Hawaiian trip affected me differed. My dad was greatly concerned. Later, looking back on that day, he thought the walk was an early hint that I had Friedreich's ataxia.

Dad: *On the trip to Hawaii, I was piggybacking Brian over the lava flows trying to get to where we could watch the molten lava cascade into the sea. Climbing over that stuff was exhausting. I ended up turning back with Brian. While Phil and Valerie pressed on, we waited by the car for what seemed like ages. Worried, I headed back to the edge of the lava flow where a lady told me that there was a mother and child struggling on the flow. She thought the boy was exhausted. Eventually, we got them back. Indeed, Phillip was wiped out—another clue we missed.*

My mom, on the other hand, was energized.

Mom: *We went to Hawaii over Presidents' Day week-end, which meant taking Phillip out of school for four days. His first-grade teacher was horrified that we would pull him out of school for something as frivolous as a Hawaiian vacation. Of course, she assumed we'd be spending our time lying on a beach. Instead, we snorkeled in Kealakekua Bay (which was like swimming in an aquarium), went deep-sea fishing, and spent a whole day on an active volcano.*

We took a helicopter ride right over the calderas and lava flows, then went for a dangerous walk. In retrospect, it was horribly stupid and I jeopardized our lives. But both Phillip and I were captivated and drawn to the spot where the lava flowed into the Pacific. Cautiously, we trudged across the hot, hard lava to the main conduit to the sea. Beneath our feet, the ground rumbled. Somehow, we made it to the edge—the same edge that would later collapse, causing a tourist to plunge to his death.

The magma flowing into the sea underneath us would trap a bubble of seawater, turning it into steam. The steam's force would then explode the magma right over our heads, where it would fall and splatter at our feet. Before beginning the arduous journey back, I managed to get a couple of amazing photos of the airborne magma. By the time we reached the road, the lava's glassy shards had trashed our shoes. Although we were worn out, we were incredibly elated. Phillip was exhausted, but that was not how he felt emotionally, and not how he remembers that day. He remembers the excitement.

As part of his "volcano experience," we bought Phillip a big reference book and a video about Kilauea. Additionally, we collected over thirty small chunks of lava (not from the park—bad luck!) to bring back to Phillip's class. When he returned to school, he presented all of it to his teacher, who completely altered her lesson plan for that day. When she asked her students for adjectives that described the lava rock, the first-graders filled up more than two whiteboards with their 'describing words'. She shared the book, showed the video, and admitted that she had been wrong about the educational value of our trip.

The first decade of my life was, and always will be remembered as, my golden years. But, in an instant, a golden life can drastically change.

ᴅᴀᴍɴᴀᴛɪᴏɴ

Damnation

My fifth-grade teacher, Mrs. Ricks, asked my mom, "What's the story with Phillip?"

My mom shouldn't have been surprised by the question. After all, both she and my dad had noticed that I had difficulty walking and balancing. I was always dragging my hand along the wall to make sure I didn't fall over.

On Tuesday, October 4, 1994, I staggered into Dr. Larese's office for one of those routine examinations. Everything was going fine until he tested my reflexes. He pulled out that funky little reflex hammer, tapped my knee, and expected my foot to jerk.

It didn't. Nothing moved.

With an incredibly awkward look on his face, Dr. Larese asked me to leave the room with one of his nurses so I could check out some game she had on a computer. I never saw the computer. I ended up in the hall, right outside his door, sitting on a freaky-looking office chair.

On the other side of the wall, Dr. Larese was laying out the diagnosis to my parents. He told them that Friedreich's ataxia is extremely uncommon, turning up in only one of every fifty thousand births. He explained to them that it was passed on to me genetically. Because it was so rare, not much was known about it. And, because it was (and still is) so rare, it was barely being researched.

My parents emerged from his little office with very, very bloodshot eyes, and the overwhelming duty of passing on to me what they had just been told.

The car ride home was otherworldly. I was only ten at the time and not fully aware of what had just been thrown at me. I wasn't sure how much FA would affect my future, but I was old enough to know that what I had was bad. When we pulled up to our house on the hill, I bolted from the car and ran into the night, screaming my head off.

It was my father who chased after me. He scooped me up and tossed me over his shoulder. Then I heard something I had never heard before. For the first time in my life, I heard my dad cry.

My parents remember that night as being dark—exceptionally dark—both literally and figuratively.

Mom: *You remember the details of the worst day of your life. They are permanently seared into your soul.*

It was raining only as it can rain in California. The clock may have read four thirty in the afternoon, but the sky was so dark you would have thought it was late in the evening. The clouds emptied their contents onto the unprepared commuters and pedestrians, who were caught off guard by such a heavy rain so early in the season.

I had just left the Fremont Main Library, and no matter how quickly the wipers cleared my windshield, I might as well have left them off. My vision was blocked more by my tears than the rain.

In 1994, there was no Internet—no Wikipedia. If you needed to look something up, you went to a library. I had just scoured Merritt's Neurology *for information about Friedreich's ataxia. What I learned shattered my world. We had just been told that our perfect and perfectly wonderful son would end up in a wheelchair and die young—probably in his early twenties.*

I photocopied the FA information—which was more a death sentence than a prognosis—and drove home to deliver it to Tim (Phillip's father). Nothing would ever be the same. Not for Phillip. Not for his younger brother, Brian, who would be forced to live beneath the shadow of Friedreich's ataxia. And certainly not for Tim and me. (Two years later, our marriage would end.) I stuffed the folded paper into Tim's hand. "It doesn't get any worse," I said.

Yet, it could have been worse. I thought about Kevin Collins. Not long before Phillip was diagnosed, Kevin disappeared from the streets of San Francisco. Fifteen years have passed, and Kevin Collins has never been found. His parents lost him. They've spent the last fifteen years wondering if he is alive or dead.

At least I still had my son. Despite the inevitable, piercing pain that I'd be forced to endure while watching Phillip deteriorate, I had to remember that it could be worse. As devastating as it was, it could be worse. It always could be worse.

My father's recollection of the evening of the day that changed everything is as painful as my mom's.

Dad: *It was a dark and stormy evening (yes, really). I was with Phillip and Brian at home. The gutters were overflowing. Valerie was at the library researching Friedreich's ataxia. I was in the garage, reaching for the ladder, ready to tackle the gutters when Valerie burst in and thrust some papers into my hands. "It's as bad as it gets," she said.*

I read the papers. There was absolutely nothing good in them to grab hold of. My son had maybe five to eight more years, and that would be it. I felt myself spiraling from normalcy to paralysis—if my heart even lasted. No treatment. No cure. No future. I went outside, into the rain. I climbed the ladder, cleaned the gutters, and cried.

Initially, at least, the diagnosis was not as devastating to me as it was to my parents. I was still naive. It was the immediate aftermath that was more troublesome. My parents shuttled me all over the Bay Area for silly appointments with stupefied doctors who examined me like I was a lab rat. It was impersonal. I still cannot recall any of the doctors' names who poked and prodded at me during the months following Dr. Larese's diagnosis.

And I won't even attempt to remember how many physicians looked at me after the initial diagnosis. It was obvious that they were bewildered. They probably had never even seen, much less treated, someone with FA. A whole bunch of student interns looked at me as well. The difference between the actual doctors and the interns was clear. The interns scribbled notes while watching me try to walk a straight line. They saw me stumble around with my wide stance and unsteady gait, reminiscent of Frankenstein's monster.

Dressed in nothing but a white hospital gown, I took a battery of standard neurological tests. They were humiliating. With and without my eyes closed, I'd try to touch my index finger to my nose. Piece of cake, right? Yet, even with my eyes open, I had a tough time. Sometimes, I would poke myself in the eye. I was so bad at it!

Not once did any doctor give me even a flicker of hope. For physicians and wannabe physicians, I became the subject of a study. I modeled the symptoms of a bizarre disease, one that most of them had never heard of or had only read about in textbooks.

ᴘᴧ ᴵᴹᴼᵞᴿᴹᴾᴵᴹᶜᵞ ᴹᴬᵞᴧᴘᴯᵞ

The Never-ending Nightmare

Mom: *Before the diagnosis, before Phillip's body began to fall apart, he was physical, emotional, social, and intellectual perfection—and I'm not the only one who felt that way. Sue Mears, Phillip's kindergarten and third-grade teacher, told me he was a "reward student"—the sort of student who was given to a teacher as a reward or to compensate for having to cope with another, more difficult student.*

As his parent, I can tell you that he was absolutely born that way. I take no credit at all. In fact, I'm grateful for not having screwed him up too much and let his amazing perfection shine. Let me share some of my deeper thoughts on the matter…

I was always aware of Phillip's "specialness," and so were other people. One night, long before the diagnosis, I watched him sleeping in the bunk bed above his brother. I was talking to God about how wonderful he is. How he is too good for this world. I suddenly had a horrible thought: What if God figures out that

He made a mistake, and that Phillip shouldn't be here after all, and he wants him back. "Don't you dare!" I said aloud to Him. "You gave him to me! So you can't have him back!"

Years went by, and I forgot about that night—until Phillip's diagnosis. Then I couldn't help but wonder if I had been prescient. For years I grappled with my lack of understanding of the "why" of Phillip's situation, and I railed against God for giving me the greatest gift a human being could ever be given and then having it taken away. I had a hard time with this.

After a long road of dialogue with God on this subject (some of it more railing than speaking), I have come to accept the possibility that Phillip volunteered for this mission. I have told him this. I've told him that he isn't just an angel metaphorically, but that he may be an actual angel. (He, of course, thinks I'm nuts.) He is too mad at God to believe that he could be on the same team…

I wasn't in the room when the doctor delivered the horrific news to my parents. Not that it would've made any difference. Later, when we got home, I asked my mom what the hell she and the doctor were talking about while I was out of the room.

When she told me, all I could do was sit in stupefying silence and listen. She gave me a basic explanation of what my life would be like. But, because FA research was so incredibly thin, it was difficult for anyone to make an accurate prediction about life expectancy. Still, the fact that anyone was even *talking* about life expectancy was disconcerting.

Yet, now, it was all so clear why...

- While walking down the hallways, I had to drag my fingertips along the walls to steady myself.

- My times for running the mile in PE were so dreadful—so much slower than everyone else's.

- I was struggling with my handwriting and why it was becoming more and more difficult to read.

- At recess, I liked playing cards more than playing on the bars.

- I struggled with the Nintendo controller. Difficult button combinations, including my "special move" had become increasingly difficult.

- Because I sometimes staggered around like I was drunk, some people made fun of me.

Yes, it was all making sense, but being just ten, I could not yet imagine what was in store for me. After all, I didn't feel any different. But the potential of the disease that had been thrust upon me was daunting.

Unconsciously, I chose self-denial. I decided not to even begin to fathom the depth to which this disability could and would progress.

Mom, however, could make no such choice...

Mom: *Because Friedreich's ataxia is so rare, Phillip became an unwitting celebrity.*

And so it began...

That Dr. Larese, a pediatrician, made the original diagnosis was remarkable. Unlike today when FA can be detected genetically, in 1994 it could only be diagnosed clinically. Back then, many Friedreich's ataxians spent years being shuffled from doctor to doctor, hearing that they were just clumsy, needed to try harder, needed to exercise more, or were given a completely incorrect diagnosis.

Dr. Larese told us that he wanted "his friend," the chief of neurology, to see Phillip. He did and concurred with the FA diagnosis.

Meanwhile, our dear neighbor, Dr. Moses Taghioff, who also happens to be a respected neurosurgeon, agreed to examine Phillip. He, too, believed it was FA and referred us to Dr. Berg, the UCSF Medical Center's chief of pediatric neurology.

We drove Phillip to San Francisco and found Dr. Berg to be a gentle, bear of a man with a head of white hair and a demeanor that added to the Santa Claus image. He put Phillip through the battery of tests that was by now becoming all too familiar:

- *The search for the deep tendon reflexes (that didn't exist).*
- *The request for Phillip to walk—or try to walk—a straight line, first with his eyes open, then with them closed.*
- *The doctor asking him to touch his index finger to his nose with his eyes closed.*

And a host of other tests, all leading to the same miserable, inescapable conclusion—Phillip had Friedreich's ataxia.

The UCSF Medical Center is a teaching hospital. Consequently, it wasn't surprising when Dr. Berg asked Phillip if he could invite some of his "friends" in to "meet" Phillip. Always agreeable, Phillip said sure. Stuck in my mind to this day is little Phillip, sitting on a stool in the middle of the crowded exam room, wearing nothing but his tighty-whities while a group of specialists stared at him like he was a celebrity. Phillip would probably be the only Friedreich's ataxian they would ever see, and they didn't want to miss the opportunity.

Dr. Berg reviewed the clinical testing and answered their questions. In an effort to be thoughtful, some of his colleagues even directed questions to Phillip. One thing was for certain: My son was no longer a typical ten-year-old.

The testing didn't stop. Friedreich's ataxia is insidious. Not only does it progressively destroy the nervous system, but it also leads to cardiac and spinal complications. Scoliosis, requiring spinal fusion surgery, is common in Friedreich's ataxians as is diabetes and other health troubles.

The three months following the diagnosis seemed like one dreadfully long doctor's appointment. Phillip saw cardiologists, had EKGs, and had echocardiograms that confirmed that he had already developed the classic cardiomyopathy associated with FA.

He began an eleven-year association with his pediatric orthopedist who would eventually identify and treat his scoliosis. He saw specialists I can't even remember, including an optometrist, an ophthalmologist, and a visual field specialist, ostensibly to establish baseline readings on every test available. I understood that they wanted to make sure no stone was left unturned. But I also wonder how many of those doctors gave Phillip their time and attention because they wanted to be able to put their hands on someone suffering with something astonishingly rare.

No longer was it just strangers in restaurants and airports who wanted to touch Phillip.

My dad's life would never be the same either. How could it have been?

Dad: *It is amazing how clearly I recall so much of it...*

Observation: When people (friends?) learn you have a child who is really sick, some shun you. It's almost like they are afraid it could be infectious, or that they could catch the bad luck. They don't want to ask how you're doing, and they have no concept of how to deal with it. So they

ignore it. Meanwhile, Phillip's mother and I were climb-
ing the walls, facing something that no parent should ever
have to face—watching a precious child suffer and slowly
die.

Friedreich's ataxia consumed our family. I'm sure that
Brian grew up thinking that Phillip was the favorite son.
After all, Phillip did get most of the attention.

We declared war on FA. There had to be something we
could do. The Internet was brand new, so I searched it and
found other sufferers of similar illnesses. We found a way to
see just about every type of doctor known to man. Regrettably,
most had never even heard of Friedreich's ataxia.

Our neighbor (and noted brain surgeon), Dr. Taghioff,
agreed to see Phillip (at no cost). He put us in touch with
specialists at the University of California, San Francisco. At
that time (1994), there was only a clinical diagnosis, but at
UCSF they confirmed the general practitioners' original specu-
lation—FA. (Years later, a fund-raiser would take place at
Dr. Taghioff's house, which was built on top of where our old
house had once stood.)

At bedtime I would lie on Phillip's bed with him for a
while and read to him. I'd rub the back of his neck, hoping
I could pull the FA out of him and into me. I did that for a
long time.

After the diagnosis, we understood why he could not run
properly, why he was clumsy, why he gave up bike riding, and
why he fatigued so easily. I had to deal with a lot of guilt.

People's reactions to me having Friedreich's ataxia would vary from wonderful to terrible. My mom's dilemma was deciding on whom to tell.

Mom: *Although the early weeks after Phillip's diagnosis seemed like we were being pulled downstream without an oar, with no control over what was happening to us, there were some decisions we had to make. Probably the most important was whom to tell about Phillip's diagnosis. There was no way we could gloss over the severity of the diagnosis to Phillip. He was, after all, an active participant in all the appointments and tests. His pediatrician reminded us that children live very much in the present, and don't worry much about the future. So we should just take advantage of that natural tendency and keep Phillip in the present. When he did ask me questions about his Friedreich's ataxia, I would deluge him with so many details that he wouldn't think I was holding anything back. Doing that allowed me to avoid telling him what the textbooks said: That he would probably be in a wheelchair in his teens and not live beyond his twenties.*

We told family about the diagnosis immediately. But what about Phillip's friends? What should we tell them? Some parents decide not to say anything to their child's peers, but we took the opposite approach. I will always be glad we did. By the time Phillip was diagnosed, he was noticeably clumsy. To leave his friends in the dark about his condition, or to expect Phillip to explain Friedreich's ataxia to everyone, would have been cruel. So, a few weeks after his diagnosis, I scheduled an appointment with his fifth-grade teacher to explain Phillip's diagnosis to his class. I was glad when Phillip didn't express any reservations.

Fortunately, Phillip's academic standing would become a factor in how Friedreich's ataxia would affect his life. In first grade he was diagnosed as "gifted." So by fifth grade, Phillip was in a classroom full of gifted and high-achieving children who had been his classmates since third grade.

It was into this environment that I brought the news of Phillip's diagnosis. As a visual prop and icebreaker, I shared his MRI films, mostly because they proved that Phillip really did have a brain! His classmates laughed, then listened attentively and curiously. I'm convinced that they took away an understanding of Phillip's condition— and that he would increasingly struggle with his balance and coordination. "Eventually," I told the kids, "he will have to use a wheelchair." If there had been any tendency to tease Phillip about his clumsiness before my classroom visit, I never heard about it. And after his classmates were gathered together and told the facts, they were unbelievably supportive.

Even Phillip wasn't aware of all the ways his peers had his back—sometimes literally. One of the other mothers remembers Phillip playing foursquare on the tarmac. On one play, when Phillip had to back up suddenly, a classmate hurried behind him, ready to catch him should he fall. When Phillip maintained his balance, his friend returned to his place without Phillip ever knowing that he had been there.

Just weeks after his classmates learned about his diagnosis, they were off on a field trip to San Francisco's Academy of Sciences. I volunteered to drive. I loaded Phillip and five other boys into our station wagon and away we went. The trip to the city was full of the usual shenanigans you would expect from a bunch of ten-year-old boys out for a day of fun and adventure. But the trip home was something else entirely.

One of Phillip's classmates asked me how Phillip "got" Friedreich's ataxia. Because I knew they had studied Mendel and his peas, I was certain they had learned basic dominant/recessive genetics. I explained that the Friedreich's ataxia gene is just like the gene for blue eyes—it is recessive. Phillip got one FA gene from me and one from his father. As one question led to another, each inquisitive, insightful, and clearly demonstrating a hunger to understand what was happening to their friend, you could have heard a pin drop in that car. I was both impressed and grateful. Impressed by the degree of understanding they displayed and grateful that we had the opportunity to talk about FA in such depth and at such length. Those five boys became the core of Phillip's growing network of friends, and they would stand by him and support him all the way through high school.

Being so young, I could not yet imagine the full scope of Friedreich's ataxia or how severely disabled I would eventually become. I regarded the diagnosis as an excuse to get out of the mile run we were required to complete in PE. I never was much of a jock, so I figured FA would allow me to spend more time pursuing my interest in art.

Thinking like a child, I naively believed I could tackle this ataxia thing. It couldn't be that much of a problem! My method for rebelling against it would be to work out, get stronger, and kick its ass. With focus and dedication, I would eventually destroy the malice of Friedreich's ataxia. I thought of myself as being "sick." Eventually, I'd get better.

I was eager to try anything to combat my condition and bust free from Friedreich's ataxia's boundaries. When family friends from Britain moved to town, they were adamant supporters of the rehabilitative possibilities of a foreign mushroom. I gave it a shot but no luck. My mother learned a great deal when she joined an online organization for parents of kids with FA She started shoving large quantities of pills down my throat every day. (I still take some of them.) They may have slowed the disease's advancement, but they sure didn't stop it. Eventually, my legs weakened and walking became a challenge. I hated the idea of being in a wheelchair, but I didn't have much choice. Getting around without it was becoming more and more difficult and dangerous.

Dad: *While in junior high school, Phillip's condition worsened noticeably. In eighth grade, he was staggering around.*

We urged him to use a wheelchair and brought it to school for him each day, but he refused to get in it. It was not until the end of eighth grade that he finally agreed to use the chair. That's when I modified it so it could carry his books and backpack. Before his eighth-grade promotion ceremony, I had my first exposure to pre-event wheelchair preparation. I arrived over an hour early to ensure that the stage was clear of obstructions so he could wheel himself across it.

But nothing could stop the slow but steady descending progression of this disorder. My doctor told me I would have a minimal life expectancy. He said I would be dead in five years.

ꞏ ꞏꞏ ꞏꞏꞏ ꞏ ꞏꞏ ꞏꞏꞏꞏꞏ

You've Got to Have Friends

As bad as it was, there was a bright side. There's always a bright side. But sometimes it's barely a shade brighter than pitch black.

Most of my classmates don't remember much about the early days after the diagnosis. The seriousness of my condition—or even that I had a condition—was lost on them. It makes sense. At first, I wasn't any different from what I had been prior to the diagnosis. And, of course, most young kids are pretty self-absorbed.

Holly (the girl who liked to chase me) remembers more than most.

I was absolutely scared. I was a little confused about what it was exactly and how I could help—if I could help. I felt a little hopeless being so young and having someone almost my age go through this. It was kind of a feeling like, "If this could happen to Phil, it could easily happen to any one of us." I remember feeling both worried and scared. I wasn't sure what was going to happen.

Another Chadbourne Elementary School buddy was Anuj Patel. (We would continue to be classmates throughout junior high and high school.) Anuj's recollection of that time is foggy.

I don't know if I can really pinpoint being scared or worried or curious about Phillip. From back in the day, what sticks with me is just knowing him. The transitions he went through often paralleled my own maturity progression—childhood innocence/observation, to inability to understand, to compassion, to true understanding...

As is the memory of schoolmate Felice Barash.

I honestly wasn't part of Phillip's life when he was first diagnosed with FA. I know we were in elementary school together, but I cannot remember our interactions at that point in our young lives and don't remember really understanding that he had a condition until we went on the eighth-grade DC trip. That was the first time I saw him in a wheelchair. That was when I started understanding the progression. Even then I did not know what FA was...probably not until high school did I truly understand what it meant and that it was something he was constantly fighting.

Whether by accident or by design, my friends never made me feel inferior or disabled. Sometimes they went out of their way to give me a hand, but they didn't make a big thing out of it. Even if it was unintentional, their treating me as if I was "normal" was good for me.

My buddy Brandon Sonn falls into that group of friends.

I remember being confused because I didn't quite understand what the diagnosis meant. It was a few years down the road before it clicked for me what having Friedreich's ataxia really meant and how it would change Phillip's life so drastically. I just saw him as a friend and that it was a part of him—although an unpleasant part. It didn't change our friendship.

As does neighbor and classmate Giancarlo Moats:

When you first showed up at Chadbourne (with your disability), you did stick out a little from the rest of the kids, but I think everyone did a good job helping you fit in. I particularly remember one day in fourth grade when you brought in some images from one of your CAT scans. If I remember correctly, it wasn't until Hopkins (Junior High), when you were spending more time in your wheelchair that I really understood how serious FA was. I was saddened, of course, but at the same time happy to see you still succeeding in school, especially later when you got to do some track and field. It now seems like a whole lifetime ago, taking our daily path to Mission (High School) every morning, rain or shine, and throwing the shot and discus on spring afternoons. (More on my track-and-field experience in the next chapter.)

Naturally, the adults in my world recognized the magnitude of my diagnosis more than my peers did—more than *I* did. Mrs. Nelson, our room mother, was one of those ubiquitous school parents who were always there. The kind of adult we take for granted until we are adults. Only then do we appreciate their selflessness. Mrs. Nelson understood.

I remember distinctly when I heard about Phillip's disease. I was working at a table for one of our many causes at Chadbourne Elementary when his mom came up to talk to me. She gave me the news, and I burst into tears and gave her a huge hug. I felt as bad for her as I did for Phillip. As a mom, you want all the kids to be happy and healthy, and it made me very sad.

qyȝɑ ȝʌp j'ʋ jɒɱ '
Crazy Shit I've Done

When a bunch of us FAers get together, we sometimes talk about why we do so many insane things. Is it
because we look at our time as limited, so we develop
a "What the hell?" attitude? Or, if we had been born
without FA, would we still be risk takers? All I know is
a disproportionate number of us seek every thrill we
can. Why doesn't everyone?

Rappelling (I)

It was overcast and miserable. Rain poured down in
bucket loads, putting me in a mood to snuggle under
a comforter and read by the fire. Instead, I had ridden
with my mom and my Boy Scout troop up to Moaning
Caverns in the Sierra foothills. I was twelve—still able
to walk reasonably well, not yet in the chair...

Braving the rain, I staggered into the visitor center and got all suited up in my rappelling gear. On my head sat an oversized yellow helmet with a little flashlight on top of it.

Just before our spelunking leader called me to the front of the line and began hooking me up, I noticed people walking around the visitor center wearing T-shirts that bragged, "I survived the plunge into Moaning Caverns." I soon realized why "the plunge" was considered such a feat. After making my way down through twenty feet of rock, the cavern opened up all around me. There was nowhere to go but two hundred feet straight down into the pit of the cave, where those who did not have the balls to rappel were milling around after having taken a spiraling steel staircase to the bottom.

Initially, I was reluctant to trust my harness. Would it hold me? I mean, it was a long way down! But after I descended a few feet, I relaxed and decided that it wasn't so bad—unless my oversized gloves managed to get wrapped up in the rappelling gear. Of course, that's exactly what happened, but I remained cool, removed the gloves and placed them on my lap until I reached the floor. When I finally got there and stood on solid ground, an overpowering adrenaline rush pulsed through my veins—the kind of moment that makes life magical.

I had to bend my neck way back to see the top of the cavern where the instructor was helping my mom who, surprisingly, had chosen to rappel down after me. Suddenly, the next kid on the line started freaking out during the transition from rock to free fall. The instructor had to race off to help him, leaving my mom. She'd have to make it down on her own. Now, inside at least, *I* was the one freaking out.

Mom: *I had no intention (or desire) to rappel with Phillip and the Scouts. I had planned to be one of those people (with no balls) who took the stairs to the bottom where I'd reconnect with brave ones and continue on with the spelunking part of our adventure. But our group's professional leader was persuasive and encouraging. He and Phillip managed to coerce me into taking the "plunge." But just as I was about to lower myself into the cavern, one of the other Scouts panicked. So, understandably, our leader had to leave me and attend to him. I'd have to continue on my own while he helped the distressed Scout overcome his fear.*

Phillip had already reached the bottom. I couldn't see him in the darkness below, but he could see me in the light above. As I swallowed my quite significant fear and entered the free-fall part of my descent, I heard Phillip's voice call up from the darkness: "It's OK, Mom. You can do it!"

That really did help, because more than anything else I didn't want to embarrass my son. So I fed my line through my

harness as fast as my hands could possibly move, and I man-
aged to make it to the safety of the bottom without completely
losing it. The moment when I felt my feet firmly back on terra
firma, and I looked up to where I had just been, was one I
won't forget. It really was, as Phillip puts it, "a rush."

Once we were all safely on the cavern floor, with the cool rock beneath our feet, part two of our adventure commenced. We were divided into six-person groups, each paired with a professional cave diver who led us into the twisting tunnels beneath the cave. The tunnels' names were threatening and unforgettable: Godzilla's Nostril, the Pancake, and the Meat Grinder. Some of the crawl spaces were uncomfortably tight, constricted enough to agitate anyone with even a hint of claustrophobia. As we wound our way deeper into the solid earth, I noticed that fans had been mounted on selected rocks to circulate the stale air.

My buddy Chris Lanier remembers it like this:

There was one section of the spelunking that was called
the Pancake. It was so flat that we had to slide through it on
our stomachs. And at one point on the journey, we were so
deep into the caves that when we turned our headlights off,
we couldn't even see our own hands when we held them six
inches in front of our own face.

We spent two hours digging our way beneath the cavern. I had never been deep into a cave before. At first, it was a little scary. But, just like with the rappelling, after a few minutes, I was able calm myself down. I've learned that most scary things are only scary for a short time. If you don't panic, if you relax and adapt, you'll be fine.

I kept on pushing through until I had almost reached the end of the last tunnel. Then I got stuck. Fortunately, one of my big scouting buddies hauled me out of the hole. I was filthy. I hadn't realized that, outside, it had continued to rain and we had been spelunking through the little rivulets that had seeped into the porous cavern. No wonder I was covered with mud and soot. We all were. That's when I took a long look at our "tour guide." He was a heavyset man. I was both perplexed and impressed that he had made it through gaps that I wasn't sure even I could squeeze through.

We still weren't done. To complete our expedition, exhausted and starving, we would have to trudge up all 235 stairs of the spiral staircase. Somehow we made it. We were presented with a cool-looking card proving we could rappel and spelunk. Literally and figuratively at the top, I plopped down and peeled off my gear and overalls, spent, but exhilarated.

Rappelling (II)

Having the guts to rappel made me feel big and bad, so I decided to do it again—this time above ground— up and down the steep cliffs of Mount Diablo State Park (a thirty-mile drive north of Fremont). This time, my dad, hoping to reassert his masculinity, came with us. Once again, I was with my Boy Scout troup, San Francisco Bay Area Council Troup 556.

Feeling more confident after having one rappelling session under my belt, I didn't pay as much attention to the instructions as I had at Moaning Caverns. My dad, on the other hand, sat next to me, rapt, with full focus and untrusting eyes glued on our instructor.

After our basic training, we were told to line up in single file. That didn't happen. We may have been scouts, but we were *boy* scouts. Trying to secure a place near the front of the line—and the edge of a cliff, 250 feet above the meadow—we playfully pushed and shoved each other. I was still walking then, albeit wobbly. The other guys were cool about it, though.

When it was my dad's and my turn, we were jammed into uncomfortable harnesses and told to "trust the rope." Probably because I had rappelled before, I could and did. I was pleasantly surprised when I discovered that rappelling down the side of a mountain was easier for me than walking. Gravity worked for me, improving my balance.

My dad, however, wasn't so sure of himself. He was obviously uncomfortable (terrified?) with the notion of trusting that a single rope could support him. Yet he was able to muster up his courage and do it. He even managed to snap a picture of me during our ten-minute decent.

Dad: *The day was warm when we—a bunch of Boy Scouts and their nervous parents—met on Mount Diablo. There was some basic training in the art of rappelling and then, just like that, we were told to go. I wasn't so sure. The shear cliff was probably seventy-five feet straight down—maybe more. Several of the scouts and even some of the parents chickened out.*

When our turn came, we roped up and over the edge we went. This was not something I would have chosen to do, but I refused to let PJ (Phillip James) see my angst. It was nerve-racking, but Phillip did not seem bothered at all. He beat me down the cliff...then he wanted to do it again! So we climbed back up the trail and rappelled down again, and again—three times in all when once would have been more than enough for me.

Each time I reached the bottom, I hung out with our group for a while. Typical of rambunctious young adolescent boys, we amused ourselves by shouting all sorts of sarcastic remarks to our scout mates as they tip-toed down the side of the mountain. It was funny and fun. Each time I made it down, a few of the older scouts sought me out to give me a high five or a friendly slap on the shoulder as a way of saying good job.

Perched on a rock at the bottom of the canyon, I had the best time watching some of the crazy, fearless people do wild stuff. There was the scout and his mom who decided to have a race down the mountainside. At the very top, they would get ready. Then one of them would yell, "One, two, three, go!" and they'd kick away from the rock. They'd drop maybe fifty feet, land feet-first against the wall, then push off again. After only four touches, they'd be on the ground.

One (only one) of the older scouts had the balls to try Australian rappelling—looking straight down at the ground while descending (as opposed to looking up at the sky). "Walking" that way down the face of "Devil Mountain," he looked like Superman. I'm glad I got to see him do it, but I wasn't interested in trying it. Even I'm not that crazy.

ᴄᴡᴘ ᴊᴡᴣᴄ
G r e a t   A m e r i c a

I blame it on the wheelchair. Until I was in one, I wouldn't have described myself as an adrenaline junkie. But the rush I felt while rappelling was addicting. So, after being permanently confined to a chair, I went looking for more, somewhere where there was easier access. Surprisingly, I found some of my best fixes at Great America, an amusement park in nearby Santa Clara. My mom and dad used to work for its owner, Paramount, designing the signs posted all over the park. When I was a little kid, I got dragged there a lot, but I didn't mind. There are worse places to be hauled off to. Besides, every year I'd score a season pass.

My first trip there without my parents was with my church youth group. Fortunately, it wasn't very organized. We were able to lose our chaperones and venture out on our own. Still, the image of me, a young teenager in a wheelchair at an amusement park, conjures images of a lonely boy having a sad time, passively sitting around, twiddling his fingers while everybody else rode the rides.

It wasn't like that, though. My friends quickly realized that by accompanying a guy in a wheelchair, they could push me to the front of the long lines at the most in-demand rides. (The trick was to enter through the exit where the ride operator, spotting my wheelchair, would allow us to cut to the front.) Naturally, this made me insanely popular with my friends, who battled over which one of them would get to be my ride partner. I almost got sick of hearing, "Phil, can I ride with you?"

I'd be lying, though, if I said I didn't sometimes use my disadvantage to my advantage. David Sheffer figured it out.

I was a couple of years younger than Phil, so I never got a chance to push him around at Great America. See, there was a kind of pecking order for pushing Phil. First, it was the pretty girls, followed by the older guys, and all the younger kids basically looked on with jealousy.

Were they using me? Hell yes! Did I care? Hell no! Did I feel bad cutting in front of people who had been waiting in line, sometimes for hours? A little. But not bad enough to wait in line if I didn't have to. (I figure there ought to be a few fringe benefits to having an incurable disease.) And, to my surprise, the people I cut in front of were usually accepting and sometimes even helpful. I never felt like I was being targeted with scorn.

From that first trip on, my friends knew that if they invited me to Great America, I'd be able to get them on all the best rides really quickly. Even so, I don't think that's the reason they went with me there. All I know is those trips are some of my best memories.

Matt Perry often went with me:

There was nothing quite like those long, warm summer days. Hanging out in the sunshine, riding the roller coasters until we were dizzy, eating carnival food until we were nauseous... There was a sense of freedom about that place. After all, we could go anywhere in the park we wanted, and when you're twelve that's a big deal.

*One thing I won't ever forget about those times is how good-natured Phil was about being constantly pushed around by his friends. Ride after ride after ride after ride! Wait. Come to think of it, Phil may have been the one pushing **us** around. I can't say whose idea it was to ride Top Gun eighteen times consecutively, but I can say that the joy was mutual. Sunup to sundown, Phil didn't get a moment of peace, but, at the same time, I don't think he offered us any. He never stopped smiling, though, not for a second. And in all the years I've known him, that's one thing that hasn't changed.*

Right. Top Gun! My favorite ride. A one-minute roller coaster full of twists and turns and upside-down flips and a special elevator for the handicapped that delivered me straight to the front of the line. No cutting required! It was always the first ride I'd ride.

When I first began frequenting Great America, I was still relatively agile. I could get up from my chair and walk to my seat on the ride. (Some of the people in line *did* get a little mad when they saw me do that!) But, as my disability progressed, my ability to walk deteriorated.

Once, Brandon Sonn, one of my more forceful friends, hoisted me out of my wheelchair and practically dragged me up two flights of stairs so I could board another favorite ride, the Tidal Wave. Speaking of water rides, Great America has one you don't even have to be on to enjoy. If you position yourself just right on a pedestrian bridge that passes over the Log Flume, you'll get splashed. Once Brandon wheeled me to that precise spot then ducked like a coward behind my chair! When the huge splash came, I was drenched while Brandon, protected by both my wheelchair and me, didn't get a drop of water on him. Used again!

He wasn't the only one. Mimi Sheffer, our youth pastor's daughter, did the same thing:

Seeing Phil's grin after getting doused with an enormous wave at Great America was one of the highlights of the trip. It was hard to feel bad for taking advantage of his wheelchair brakes because he was laughing so hard! I got bruises on the tops of my feet from running so fast while pushing him that I kicked his anti-tip wheels over and over again, but I was having too much fun to slow down.

Those were days I wish could have lasted forever—being teenagers, the adrenaline rush, the feeling that came from being with the most epic group of friends who ever lived. We were all sunburned for weeks after, but it was completely worth it. For a few hours, having fun was all that mattered, and it was so easy to live like we would never be sick, we would never be sad, and we would never be afraid of losing each other.

I can picture Phil standing from his wheelchair and walking to the rides without help. Looking back, I realize that, as a teenager, I was totally unable to comprehend what FA would do to his body over time, and how very serious it was. I don't know if I could have dealt with the grief of knowing it at that age, but it puts me more in awe of Phil and his family. Their strength and courage in the face of overwhelming facts still inspires me.

Mimi's mom, Marylee Sheffer, was not only our youth pastor; she was the youth group leader of our Great America trips:

Marylee: *Phil could have fun in a paper bag! I remember my son, David, telling me how cool it was to cut to the front of the line with him. What Phil describes as "not very organized" is what I call "building relationships." I know Phil has his* *doubts about God, but he shouldn't have any doubts that he was loved at youth group. That was my goal, because love is the bottom line. It's why we're here. It's what we leave behind. It's what lasts. It's what changes us. (See what happens when you ask a pastor to comment on something?) Great America? It was a great time for you guys and fun for me, too.*

Today, still, riding a thrill ride gives me a rare, special moment when I'm freed from my reality. When I'm soaring high and moving at great velocity, I'm completely healthy. There is no Friedreich's ataxia. That's why, whenever a ride ends, I'm reluctant to return to the captivity of my little wheelchair.

ᛞᛟᛗᛁ
Skiing

When I was seventeen, Brianne Konanz, who's also cursed with Friedreich's ataxia, told me that she and a group of fellow wheelchair users—not all, but most, afflicted with FA—regularly caravanned up to Lake

Tahoe for three-day skiing sessions (as ridiculous as that sounds). She asked if I'd like to join them.

Pack a hecka buncha "stuff," stick it in the back of my truck with Brianne's monster power chair, drive five hours (if it's not snowing) into the Sierras to the seven-thousand-foot level at Truckee and unload everything (including Brianne) into the cabin. It's Friday night—we're there! For the next two days, the TABs (Temporarily Able Bodied) and I sweat, grunt, work, and hyperventilate—we're at seven thousand feet! Why do I do it? Duh! Because I enjoy watching these people, who happen to be disabled, enjoy skiing! They deserve it, and I'm glad to be a part of it. At the end of the weekend I am done, toasted, finished. It takes several days to recoup.

—Paul Konanz (Brianne's father)

I had never been skiing, and, until Brianne suggested it, I hadn't even considered skiing. Then I started to wonder whether sliding down slopes might be yet another way to get that adrenaline rush I so savor. So I joined the trek to Tahoe City, California, where, nestled into the western shore of Lake Tahoe, is the Alpine Meadows Adaptive Ski School run by Disabled Sports USA (DSUSA), Far West.

When a DSUSA instructor called my name, I was "good nervous"—excited, alive, and...terrified! I had no idea what I was getting into. Before I could change my mind, I was strapped into a bucket seat mounted on skis and shoved outside into the damp snow (the packing kind that's good for making snowballs and building snowmen), where they ran me through a series of maneuvers. They taught me to lean left to turn left and lean right to turn right—pretty simple stuff. They assured me that they'd always be right behind me, holding on to me, so I wouldn't go barreling down the hill uncontrollably.

At first, I sucked. I'd lose my equilibrium and the bucket seat contraption would topple over. That first year, it was like riding a bicycle with training wheels. I was, in essence, held onto by a leash. The instructors never let me get more than a few feet away. Despite that, I enjoyed my little circuits around the course, but I rarely surpassed Meadow Run, the second beginner's course. I wasn't at all discouraged. On the contrary, I knew that skiing was for me when, even after wiping out, I'd come up laughing. Despite being a struggling beginner, I had an extremely good time. Flying down the slopes, even if a bit awkwardly, was exhilarating and addicting. On ski days, there was hardly time to eat, but I didn't care. A little bit of hunger was a fair price for pure fun.

Initially, I didn't use "outriggers"—little ski poles you hold that help you balance. I stuck with shifting my body weight from side to side. But after I gained experience, I decided to give outriggers a try. They ended up being more encumbering than helpful. They threw off my balance, so I chucked them. Which was just as well, because trying to fit my fingers into the gloves I'd have to wear to hang onto them was practically impossible. So now I just jam my fists into mittens.

Since the onset of FA, my core has been sort of floppy and hard to control. So you'd think that turning on skis would be a major challenge. Yet, surprisingly, more than once, my instructors have commented, "Phil, you have excellent balance!" Considering that balance is almost always adversely affected by Friedreich's ataxia, I have no explanation for why or how I have been able to stay upright on skis. I guess it's just one of those weird, unexplainable things. And guess what? I'm still improving. I've made it as far as the fifth chairlift. It's important, I believe, to have pursuits that you're working at to get better. For me, one of those pursuits is skiing. I'm passionate about it, and I'm not alone.

I have cerebral palsy and I've had it since birth. For me skiing is about feeling free. When I'm out on the slopes I'm not thinking about my disability. I'm thinking, "This is awesome. If I can do this, I can do anything!" The chance to do something that I never thought possible before I started going on these trips makes me want to go out and experience more new things.

—Callie (a ski buddy)

Besides the actual skiing, I look forward to having conversations with my instructors while we ride the lifts. Sometimes they'll share stories about other disabled skiers and the crazy stunts they'll pull. Compared to them, my skiing is pretty tame. I'd be lying if I said I wasn't envious. It's apples and oranges, though. I have a neuromuscular disorder while they have "only" spinal cord injuries. Even skiers who are paralyzed from the waist down are able to control their upper bodies. Their ability to navigate the slopes is much better than those of us with neuromuscular disabilities. I can only dream of roaring down a run on my own, skiing free of instructors. Reality, however, wakes me up and warns me that if I tried to do what they do, I wouldn't get far before deep-sixing it into the snow.

I relate to being a little jealous of the spinal injury guys and gals. They make it look so easy while I (we perhaps) am left bailing face first into the snow all day. The thing I love about the ski trips is that we are united by sport. I mean, c'mon, who thought a group of disabled kids would ever be on the ski slopes. It's not logical. But we bail together, we freeze together, and we shred together. It's something we can share. We all have different experiences on the slopes, but the bigger picture is that we share this sport and it makes us closer. We are connected by skiing. Who would've thought?

—Kyle Bryant, also afflicted with late-onset Friedreich's ataxia

At the end of each session, we dust the snow off our laps and pile into our vehicles for the drive back to a cabin in nearby Truckee. We always stay at the same place. Frankly, I'm astonished that they keep letting us come back. We bang around the place in our wheelchairs and totally demolish the poor doorframes.

In spite of arming myself with battery-powered electric socks, chemical hand warmers, foot warmers, and body warmers, by the end of the day, I still feel like a block of ice. Safe inside the cabin, I instantly stick my feet into my precious vibrating electric foot warmer (one of those fancy Brookstone gadgets) then down several cups of hot chocolate. Later, we eat a spaghetti dinner and collapse into our sleeping bags.

What I love about the February Tahoe trips the most is getting to hang out with the amazing people I meet there. Especially when we get back to the cabin (when all our feet are numb from a rush on the slopes), drinking hot chocolate and sharing stories is the highlight of the trip.

—Sophia Sieber-Davis—nineteen-year-old ski trip buddy (also with FA)

As with most of my adventures, it's more about the people than the activity. On nearly all of our ski trips, someone new joins us, and it's not unusual for couples in our group to fall in love. Most of us have FA, so it's interesting and motivating when I get to share time with others who are battling what I'm battling. Brianne, more than anyone, inspires me. Her FA is severely progressed. She relies on a power wheelchair to get her around. She can no longer project her voice, so it's hard to understand her when she talks. Without help, she can no longer go to the bathroom or get out of bed. Yet she skis with us. She exemplifies a kind of courage I can only hope to duplicate.

Skiing confirms that I can do what I want to do. It reminds me that I can do anything...well almost. It's funny, but a big part of the ski trip is Saturday night, staying up, drinking, playing games, or watching movies, whatever we feel like, regardless of our limitations.

—Brianne

Swimming

From the beginning—I think it started while I was still in the womb—I've loved the water. A month before I was born, my mom was sitting in our pool with my grandma, and I must have decided that I wanted to join them because I picked that moment to stick my foot through the amniotic sac. A few hours later I was born.

When I turned three, we moved into a new house where my dad built a hot tub in our backyard. Under an arbor, set in a redwood deck, it was gorgeous. I was in there all the time. Protected from the sun, it was just the right depth for my brother and me to safely relax and play for as long as we wanted—which was usually a long, long time.

The spa was great for all kinds of recreation, and not just for splashing around in the water or playing with floating toys. Imagine being the size of a four-year-old, balancing on a seat, facing the jets. Can you picture where the jet was hitting? I discovered the fun of that spot and spent lots of time with my eyes rolled back in my head, enjoying the sensation of that distinctive recreational activity. One balmy evening, I was in there with my big sister Nicola, who was visiting from England, and I started doing my thing. Noting my glazed eyes, she asked, "Philip, what are you doing?!" It wasn't as if I was going to be honest with her…Yeah, the hot tub was one of my first water "sports."

My mom's answer was to enroll me at Fremont Swim School, where I would learn to actually swim. Fremont Swim is one of those assembly-line swim schools, but it did teach me the basics. Because I was already uncommonly comfortable in the water, it didn't take me very long to master the simple art of clasping my outstretched hands over my head, pointing myself toward the opposite end of the pool, and kicking until my fingers touched the other side. Only then would I take a breath of air. I must have been fairly good at it, because I remember standing on the winner's podium after one of our school's competitions. At the time, I had no clue it would be one of the last times I'd ever win at anything athletic.

Still, swim school hardly represented real-life swimming. That I got at Becky and Patrick's house, because they had a pool. Becky was our lifeguard. Her brother, Patrick, my brother, Brian, and I were forever leaping and diving into water, competing to see who could produce the biggest splash. It would have been fine if it had been just the three of us. But, if any if our parents were sitting poolside, under the illusion that they'd be able to enjoy a relaxing moment or two, they were definitely in the wrong place. Inevitably, one of them would be doused with water.

To prepare them, we came up with a code word: *cowabunga*! (At the time, obviously, the Teenage Mutant Ninja Turtles were at the apex of their popularity, especially with young boys.) We got exceptionally good at shouting "COWABUNGA!" at the top of our lungs, catapulting ourselves into the deep end, and laughing out loud when our frustrated parents scurried to safety.

I liked to sink to the bottom of the pool and hold my breath down there for what felt like hours. Then, ever so slowly, I'd return to the surface and take a huge gulp of oxygen. Although I hadn't been diagnosed yet, one of the reasons I loved swimming was, when I was immersed in water, I wasn't clumsy. When you have balance issues like I have, water is the great equalizer. Even after the diagnosis, I didn't feel "different" when I was in the pool. Water comforted me.

It wasn't all good. (What is?) I've had some negative experiences with water.

Each summer, I'd make the trek to Camp Royaneh, the beautiful Boy Scout camp located in the heart of the Sonoma County redwoods in Russian River country. At the beginning of the session, all campers were required to undergo a swimming skills test. When it was my turn, just as I reached the middle of the pool, I completely freaked out. I gasped for air and, to hold myself up, grabbed the floating lane marker. A lifeguard extended a pole to me. I latched on and he pulled me to safety. Still, from that day on, I refused to set foot in the Camp Royaneh pool, even when the temperature reached one hundred.

Another camp pool was at Silver Spur, our church's family camp.

The first few years I was confined to my chair, I avoided the water. Getting into and out of it was too much of a hassle. Transferring from chair to pool and then from pool to chair was a major ordeal. Why even bother? But one sweltering afternoon, a bunch of my fellow campers didn't give me a choice. They lifted me out of my chair, carried me into the water and placed me on top of one of those inflatable rings.

The lifeguard on duty was Morgan. I don't remember this happening, but people tell me that I fell asleep and began to slip through the ring. Like a bullet, Morgan dove from her chair into the water and came up under me. She lifted my head above water so quickly that I didn't even cough. But even though I got to be rescued by an attractive chick, I was so embarrassed that I never set foot in that pool again, either.

Today, both my mom and dad have pools at their homes, and I'm not afraid to swim in either of them. But not only do I need help getting into and out of the water, I need someone to remain with me in the pool, too. I can't lift my head above the water without assistance—which definitely sucks. Luckily, thankfully, I have lots of energetic friends who will visit me, take me swimming, and watch over me.

ᴀᴘ ᴊᴇ ᴄᴍᴄᴊ

Waterskiing

**Fortunately, I've found alternate ways to
enjoy water.**

In addition to snow skiing, Disabled Sports USA offers
waterskiing. So, the year I turned eighteen, I decided
to give it a try. Because water doesn't support you
nearly as securely as snow does, skiing on a lake is a

hell of a lot harder than skiing on a hill. On the other hand, falling into warm water is a lot less painful than crashing into the icy snow.

For me, the water "ski" is really a wakeboard with a seat attached to it. That first summer, every time I tried it, I fell. I hardly minded, though, because we always skied in California's scorching Central Valley where the cool water felt divine. Even so, not being able to get "up" was frustrating.

So I returned the next summer for more. Eventually, after dozens of tries, I finally got up. What a feeling of accomplishment. Making turns was tricky, but I found a way to do it. I'd pull the towrope from its slot on the ski tip and, while grabbing hold of it with all my strength, manage to stay up for a couple of circuits around the lake. It was incredibly gratifying. The best kind of natural high.

Anyone who waterskis knows that, even if it's not considered a team sport, it certainly requires a group effort. Someone has to drive the boat and someone else has to spot the skier—look out for him or her, especially in the event of a fall. When that happens the spotter raises a flag and the driver circles the boat and retrieves the downed skier.

For me to ski, the group of three has to be expanded to a group of five. Two additional volunteers have to be with me in the water: one to help position me prior to the boat pulling me forward, the other on a Jet Ski ready to follow me, in case I go down. I don't mind the extra help. The volunteers are usually hot girls, which makes the help I get after falling over even more pleasurable than the refreshing water.

aλp-apý yѣpṁ_u
White-Water Rafting

This book isn't a plug for Disabled Sports USA—well, maybe it is—but DSUSA also leads white-water rafting trips. Naturally, I wanted to try that, too. Anything in or on the water excites me. So, about the same time I began waterskiing, I went rafting on the American River's class III rapids. Since my mom and my brother, Brian, could join me, it was a cool, bonding type of family adventure.

There were two raft groups in our party. The other group chose to take the calm, meandering course. Mom, Brian, and I went for the wild ride. There's a scene in the Disney movie *Pocahontas* where she's rowing her canoe down a river, and she comes to a fork. She has to make a choice between taking the safe, comfortable but less exciting path or the risky, scary but more rewarding part of the river. Like Pocahontas, I tend to go for the high-risk/high-reward selection. Would I be like that if I didn't have FA? I don't know. I really don't.

Anyway, we weren't at all afraid, so our guides helped us steer through the river's most challenging rapids, hoping to give us the best adventure possible. They succeeded. I didn't have any kind of special chair. I was just sitting on the bottom of the raft, without much support. I remember being thrashed around quite a bit. But hearing the rapids roar, feeling the water slam into us and seeing a look of utter thrill spread over my brother's face made it worth it—even the torturous sunburn I had to endure afterward.

I didn't raft again until 2010. The American River had been fun, but this time it was the big league—the Colorado River. I went with a group called Splore (a Utah nonprofit that provides outdoor adventures for people with disabilities). Four other Friedreich's ataxians and their families joined us. Unlike the day trips I took with DSUSA, this was a big deal—a five-day trip.

We spent our nights on the Colorado's sandy shores. After rafting all day, the Splore staff and volunteers would unpack everything from our rafts and set up camp. And when I say "everything," I mean *everything*. They even brought a makeshift toilet they called the "Groover." An environmentally correct trip all the way, we couldn't leave *anything* behind! Teaching us to respect, appreciate, and look after nature is an important part of Splore's mission.

One of my favorite Splore staff members, Claire Hay, shared with me her perspective.

Before working at Splore, I had spent a few years volunteering with adaptive programs for people with developmental disabilities and had felt incredibly fulfilled by those experiences. So, when I found out about a chance to work at Splore for the summer, I applied, kind of on a whim. When I started working for Splore, I had no idea what I was getting myself into. Not only had I never professionally river guided before, but my experience with adaptive recreation was, I would come to find out, limited at best.

The five-day FA trip down Ruby Horsethief/Westwater Canyon was really the defining point of my summer. From the first few hours on the river, I was impressed by the energy and enthusiasm of every participant. Those who could paddle were trading turns in the sit-on-top kayak, while others were excited to float alongside the rafts, even if they didn't have previous river experience. I was impressed because I know that the river, which is murky at best, could be a little daunting, but no one hesitated to get into the water.

By our final day, when we hit the rapids, I felt like I had come to know everyone on the trip on a new level, one that I don't think is possible to experience between two people who don't know what it's like to have a disability. Being around so many people, some my age or even younger, who, every day, are forced to deal with more obstacles than I have in my entire life, was humbling. The FA trip really taught me that I can do so much that I take for granted. In some ways, it also made me realize that I can feel so much more humbled by what I CAN do than by what I can't.

Despite the Colorado's reputation for white-water adventure, the focus of this trip wasn't so much on the thrill of the rapids as it was on the quality of the friendship they hoped we'd forge. Initially, the thought of spending five days tucked in a raft with a bunch of strangers, even strangers with FA, concerned me. What if they were boring? What if they were annoying? Would I have any privacy? Even though I had already met some of them and considered them friends, knowing people and living with people in intimately close quarters is an entirely different experience.

It turned out that my worries were unwarranted. I enjoyed being on the river with other Friedreich's ataxians and their families. Even the Splore people, who had come for our benefit, seemed to enjoy the adventure almost as much as we did. Almost instantly, I developed memorable friendships with the new people and cemented relationships with old acquaintances. Except for our parents, everyone was my age or younger, so, in addition to our coping with FA, we had a lot in common and much to talk about.

In eighth grade, my US history teacher taught us that on the Mayflower, all 102 passengers were crammed into one cabin. People had to pee and poop in a bucket, right in front of everyone. Privacy was not an option.

That's how I felt on this trip. The Groover couldn't be set up in some distant location. Because we were all mobilely challenged, everything had to be close, so close it was. At each stop, a three-sided tent was erected to provide privacy. Usually, the open side provided the potty user with a grand view of the river. So, while we were doing our business, we were secluded from those in *our* group. But pity the poor person using the Groover when some other unsuspecting, soon-to-be-surprised, rafting party floated by.

For me, conquering the Groover turned out to be one of the major challenges and indignities of the trip. For three days, by the time my mom and two other volunteers managed to haul me from wherever I was when nature called to the Groover (and get me into fighting position), the urge had passed. Everyone knew what was going on, and many of the adults had tried to help me, but all attempts had failed. So, "beating the clock" became a camp-wide obsession.

Then, finally, on morning number four, we succeeded. The instant I felt the urge, I woke up my mom. Two able-bodied people scooped my naked body out of my sleeping bag. (Hey, especially when I'm camping, I prefer sleeping in the nude!) They hustled me past a group of campers who were relaxing on canvas chairs, sipping their morning coffee. They continued through our makeshift kitchen, where the staff was preparing a wonderful blueberry pancake breakfast. Hurriedly, they placed me onto the Groover, where success was met and announced to all. A hearty cheer resounded throughout the camp. Then, with my male parts bouncing around for everyone to see, I was lugged back to my tent while I received high fives and congratulations along the way.

Around the house, Mom and I aren't into toilet humor. We don't crack bathroom jokes. So we were caught off guard a little when we discovered that the humor of this group had no boundaries of taste. Both in camp and on the river, bawdy jokes about body parts abounded. Realizing that it would be impossible to live in such intimate quarters and be a prude, we adapted. We quickly learned that everybody on the trip had some form of weirdness about them. There were the insane dancing breast implants on our program manager's chest. (She claimed she could make them move independently and—after a little coaxing—she felt comfortable enough around us to prove it!) And I'll never forget the wild dreadlocks that streamed from the head of our program coordinator.

The humor served a purpose. I've found that you can joke most freely with your closest friends and family members, and the Splore staff associates seemed more like brothers and sisters than coworkers. Despite the coarse humor (later, because of it), we were honored when the bizarre Splore staff involved us in their humor and included us in their family.

When our rafts slowed and there were no rapids in sight, both passengers and crew took turns hurdling jokes, riddles, and playful insults back and forth. We played mind games about a wide variety of subjects. Because it helped us learn so much about each other, the ceaseless banter made us closer.

I may have Friedreich's ataxia, but I'm still a guy who likes girls, and it seems like there has always been a girl. On this trip, her name was Keegan Athey. Keegan was one of the Splore volunteers. She took the time to really listen to what I had to say, which takes a great deal of patience. She took the time to get me out of the boat and onto the river where we'd float along, exploring, while the penetrating Utah sun beat down on us. We kept hydrated, played games, made our signature Splore tie-dyed shirts, and got to know each other intimately well.

Unfortunately, Keegan had a boyfriend. (Don't they always?) So I wouldn't allow myself to get *too* big a crush on her. Even so, I sure missed her after she kayaked out of camp because, as she phrased it, she had "an obligation elsewhere." The good-bye hug and kiss she gave me the night before she left will stay with me forever.

As we made our way down the river, we mourned the passing of two rafters who had been on this same trip a year earlier. One of them had been a Splore client. Tragically, she had died in camp. She had been seriously ill for a long time and her heart finally gave out. The other was an FAer named Keith Andrus-Bartek. He was the first Friedreich's ataxian I ever met. He had lost his battle with FA the previous January. I don't get choked up very often, but those memorials were an exception. Not only did I feel the obvious impact of losing people I cared about deeply, but I also was profoundly affected by emotional reactions others displayed during the memorial. Most of the Splore staff and all the FAers were sobbing. It felt peculiar to be immersed in a group of people, some younger than I, who were so deeply moved by their losses. I couldn't help but feel that as much as the tears were for the others, some of them fell for us. As I write this, I do so in the shadow of the recent passing of yet another FAer, Aaron Kittel—the cornerstone of our rafting trips. Aaron started rafting with his family years ago. His younger brother became one of the staff river guides. He has organized an annual FA rafting trip for several years now. I don't mean to sound overdramatic, but it's a very real truth: the shadow of death lurks near all of us who live with Friedreich's ataxia.

Fellow rafter Jamie Plourde posted this comment on my Facebook wall:

I was thinking back about the 2010 rafting trip, and the one thing that stuck in my memory was when you first told me about the book you were writing. I thought it was such an inspiring idea, something I'd like to read. It really broke my heart when you said you hoped the book would be finished before you died. You were so honest about the situation, and it made me think about what life would be like if you were terrified each day and the importance of living each and every day.

(Jamie is special and great. During the early stages of her FA, she was named Miss Wheelchair New Hampshire. I have to admit, she's pretty cute. She went on to attend Keene State College in Keene, New Hampshire.)

Our adventure ended on a scary, thrilling but (thankfully) high note. The last day was rapids day. The Splore staff seemed a little uptight and intense. To me, though, it was just a day of thrills. To them, it was a day of huge responsibility, truly a matter of life and death. Because of the previous year's tragic in-camp death, last year's group never made it to the rapids.

Understandably, a ton of emotional weight was brought to the rapids, but I didn't feel it at first. Brad Woodford, our dreadlocked raft guide, was unusually quiet that morning. He had the awesome responsibility of ensuring that all nine of our rafts made it safely past the exhilarating, yet terrifying rapids. I learned later that every year someone perishes in those rapids!

Naturally, extreme precautions were taken. I wasn't allowed to be strapped into my chair. Instead of the usual one person watching over me, two people held onto me. If our raft capsized, I could die! The Splore staff took every measure to protect me. They promised that they weren't going to let anything happen to me on *their* watch.

Not unlike our guide had done on the DSUSA trip all those years before, Brad tried to give us the biggest thrills he could while still keeping us safe. He succeeded. Still, there was one rapid where we were all so perilously airborne that we easily could have come down on the raft's edge and toppled into the water. Luckily, we landed inside the raft and upright. So, drenched to the skin but with huge smiles plastered on our faces, we pushed onward! When the last rapid was successfully passed and we were safely floating on calm water, Brad stood up, let out a loud whoop, and joyfully dove into the Colorado—his way of celebrating our victory.

Rapids day was a reflection of the entire trek's success. It successfully brought a group of people to nature—real, wild, rip-roaring nature—where we did stuff we hadn't ever even dreamed of doing. It successfully gave us the kind of life-enhancing jolt we can't get in our day-to-day lives. Maybe more important, it successfully made a bunch of people who normally feel like misfits, fit.

For a few days, *normal* was sitting in a wheelchair. *Normal* was needing someone to hold your cup for you and feed you. *Normal* was having a hard time speaking clearly enough to be understood. *Normal* was having a blast playing board games, even when you need someone else to throw the dice. *Normal* was cracking jokes, even though it took a while to get the words out. And *normal* was laughing and crying together, as if we had known each other all our lives.

S k y d i v i n g

"Remember when sex was safe…And Skydiving was dangerous?"

From a bumper sticker I put on my bedroom wall.

The first time I seriously considered skydiving was when I saw photographs—actual proof!—of Brianne skydiving. It wasn't just that she had done something I hadn't. (My whole life has been about watching friends do things I can't.) It was because Brianne has FA! So, even though I'm stuck in a wheelchair, I knew skydiving was something I *could* do. And, deep inside, I knew it was something I would love. I imagined skydiving would be like Great America's Drop Zone, only amplified a thousand times. An amusement park ride on steroids.

Even though I've skydived six times, my first time was my best time. (I hear that applies to other things, too.) In July 2003, as a birthday present from my parents, I got to go to Skydive Santa Rosa (which operates out of the tiny Charles Schulz Sonoma County Airport). Brianne had recommended them, so we knew that they had experience with people like me.

This is what it's like to tandem skydive: You're securely strapped to the chest of an experienced skydiving instructor, then, together, you drop into space. The parachute is attached to the instructor's back, and you're strapped to his front...

Wait, I'm getting ahead of myself here. Before you get to jump out of the plane, you have to jump through hoops. First, you read and sign a bunch of liability release forms. Even though skydiving is surprisingly safe, you still have to sign so many forms you'd swear you were agreeing to swim with tiger sharks. Next, to see what you're in for, you watch a video of someone else skydiving. This is so, if necessary, you can gracefully back out while you're still on the ground.

Three macho guys ahead of me (at least that's how I originally pegged them) did just that. Right after they saw the video, they changed their minds and left. On me, it had the opposite effect. *Hell yes!* I thought. *Let's do this!*

One reason I wasn't afraid was because my orthopedist had reassured me that I could handle a harsh landing. Even though the hardware they put in my back (when they fused my spine) had broken in one place, he wasn't worried about it getting any worse. So neither was I.

After the skydiving staff geared me up, they wheeled me to the airplane, leaving behind my chair—and all it represents. I was lifted into the plane and attached to my instructor. Our assent leveled out at twelve thousand feet. Somebody unlatched the door. I was given one last chance to chicken out. I didn't.

The moment we jumped from the plane, my stomach jumped into my throat. I was utterly terrified, yet, strangely, it wasn't a bad terror. It was a fantastic thrill, one I'll never, ever forget. We somersaulted a few times before Doug, my instructor and tandem partner, pulled the "drag chute" (a miniparachute that keeps you level, while limiting velocity to "only" 120 miles per hour). I was surprised to find myself consciously enjoying the matchless rush.

While we plummeted toward the rapidly approaching earth, the wind sucked in my cheeks and ripped back my hair. We had fallen nine thousand feet before Doug yanked open the primary chute, immediately and drastically slowing us. I have to tell you, when that chute opens, it jerks you! Doug was prepared, though. He held my forehead so that the jolt wasn't too stressful on my neck. After peacefully floating the final three thousand feet, my parents with my wheelchair and all it represents were waiting. Thankfully, Mom and Dad had hired a videographer to jump with us, so I have it all documented.

I admit it. Not only am I addicted to the physical kick skydiving unfailingly delivers, I relish the admiration I get from nonskydivers, often people who are bigger, stronger, and more physically capable than I. Neither of my parents have skydived, nor has my brother. Almost everyone who watches my skydiving video squirms in their seat when they see us tumble out of the airplane. One unexpected exception was my grandmother. "I'd love to do that!" she announced. Realistically, I don't see that happening, but who knows? What do I know about "realistic"?

Although most people tell me there's no way they'd jump out of a perfectly good airplane, FAers don't think like most people. Brianne, for example, has skydived more than two dozen times, and she's not alone. It's not unusual to meet an FAer who has skydiving experience. Many have multiple jumps.

Why is that? The United States Parachute Association estimates that less than 1 percent of Americans have skydived. So, why is it that at least a quarter of the FAers I know are skydivers? And for many of those who haven't yet tried it, the reason they haven't isn't reluctance. It's either that they don't have close enough access to a skydiving airport or that they just can't afford it. So many of them say, "Oh, I want to do that *so* badly!"

Does the struggle just to get through each day make FAers more fearless? Does being captive in our wheelchairs make us hungry for the ultimate physical freedom? Are we drawn to doing something that almost no one else has done because it defines us in some way other than wheelchair-bound? Or do we just think, *What the hell? Life's short. Why not go for it?*

Probably all of those. For me, the nine thousand feet of free fall are the best seconds I know. Because during those ephemeral moments, I'm free. And strong. And brave.

And *soooo* happy!

ρΛγᾶῖ̃ᾳ
Throwing

Just for kicks and because my friends talked me into it, I tried out for the Mission San Jose High School track-and-field team. No, I didn't race around the track in my wheelchair. Neither did I somehow manage to pitch myself out of it far enough to qualify for the long jump (although I have accidently pitched myself out of it so often, if there *was* an Olympic sport in wheelchair pitching, I'd be ready for it.) I earned my letter throwing the shot put and discus.

I use the term "tried out" loosely. Truth is, nobody gets cut from track. It, along with a handful of other sports teams—swimming, cross-country, badminton—will take anybody. You may not get to compete in the event(s) you want—actually, there's no guarantee you'll get to compete at all—but at least you'll be on the team.

I thank Dane Lentz and Giancarlo Moats for convincing me to join the team. During my junior year, to fulfill my physical education credits, I was working out in the weight room. The track-and-field athletes were bulking up, including the "throwers." Dane and Giancarlo, the two main throwers, encouraged me to come out. I was surprised when the coaches let me join. Luckily, track is one of those sports in which the team score isn't averaged out, so my complete lack of ability didn't bring down the rest of the team. In fact, my nonexistent ability seemed to actually bring the team up.

For some Mission students, much to the consternation of their more serious teammates, the only motivation to join track is that, supposedly, it looks good on the "résumé." They think it will help them get into college.

I say that's a shitty reason to do anything, and even though I wanted to get into college, "because it will spice up my college application" certainly wasn't my motivation to go out for track. I just wanted to meet people and have fun.

Still, it wasn't an easy decision. I went through a "try-out-for-something" version of the "five stages of grief." (From Elisabeth Kubler-Ross's landmark study and book, *On Death and Dying*, 1969.) Not unlike what I (and, to a greater extent, my parents) experienced after my diagnosis, before trying out for track, I was in stage one: denial. "There is no way I can do this sport." In the end, curiosity got the best of me. "*Could* I do this?" So I signed up and forced myself to get out there.

Immediately, I felt inferior. I couldn't run or jump, so my only choice was to throw. I became a shot put and discus guy. A field guy. The problem was, because my teammates' throws soared like ten times farther than mine, I felt frustrated and angry (grief's second stage). Often, I was pissed off, and, sometimes, I'd take it out on my teammates.

Let's face it. Track and field is tough for anyone, but for me it was brutal.

I mean, you'd think that throwing the shot six or seven feet couldn't hurt anything other than what it landed on, but it turned out it wasn't completely without risk. One afternoon, after my mom picked me up from practice, I wasn't feeling at all well. My heart was racing like it was in the Daytona 500. I was in a cold sweat and felt like throwing up. When Mom got me home, she took my pulse. It was some crazy high number, so, somewhat freaked, she rushed me to the ER.

This turned out to be my most serious heart episode. I was in atrial fibrillation. The ER staff shifted into high gear. They presumed I was having a heart attack—a myocardial infarction. My cardiac enzymes, produced by a heart in stress, were at levels "consistent with a fatal heart attack." So I ended up spending a couple of days in the cardiac intensive care unit. This was another of those times in the hospital when I watched my parents use humor to cope with a crisis. They'd cut each other up with dumb jokes. One time, they used the oxygen sensor attached to my finger to turn the display monitor into something like an Etch A Sketch. At one point—in the ER, no less—a nurse on the other side of the curtain sarcastically suggested that they were "having way too much fun in there!" Even though I understood that it was Mom and Dad's coping mechanism, that was a time I could have lived without their lame jokes.

So there I was in the ICU. They pumped me with drugs hoping to slow my heart while, at the same time, monitoring it to make sure it wouldn't go into fibrillation again. Meanwhile it was time for the track-and-field team photo, and I really didn't want to miss it. So I asked my cardiologist if I could leave the hospital for a couple of hours so I could be included in the photo. He scolded me, pointing out that, "If you are well enough to leave the ICU, you are well enough to be moved to the general hospital ward, but you *never* get discharged from the ICU to go home. That's just not the way it goes."

Mom wasn't buying it. As I well know, she can be pretty damn persuasive. Eventually, after purchasing a blood pressure monitor and promising the doc that she'd take my pulse and blood pressure every hour, he released me. I left the hospital and went straight to school for the photo. When the guys found out where I had been, they were openly concerned. It's always nice to know people care. Have you ever been absent from school and, when you returned, nobody even knew you had been gone? Makes you feel irrelevant, right?

Anyway, a few days later, my cardiologist cleared me to return to throwing with one crucial condition: I could stay on the team provided I stopped weight training. He put it something like this: "Phil, I want you to take care of your heart so that you live, but I also want you to have a life."

I loved that.

The third stage of grief—bargaining—wasn't really an option for me. It would have meant making some sort of deal to get better (on so many levels). But since neither a cure nor steroids were an option (even if I shot up, they wouldn't have helped), I trudged from bargaining into stage four: depression.

"I suck at this. I look like an idiot. Why even bother?" To my eternal gratitude, however, whenever I found myself in despair, my teammates (by then, my friends) and coaches reassured me. "You deserve to be here, Phil! Nobody deserves it more than you!" And the encouragement never ceased. "You got this, Phil! Great throw! Keep trying!"

With that kind of encouragement, sometime during my second season, I was able to reach stage five: acceptance. I still sucked, but, because I was competing more for the love of the sport and to experience the kind of camaraderie that's hard to find anywhere other than in athletic settings, sucking was OK. Well, not really. Deep inside, I hated it. But I learned to live with it. Don't we all have to learn to live with and accept things we despise (but can't change)?

Nevertheless, at two different meets, I was able to score a point for my team. In track, to score, you have to place in the top three. First-place finishers earn their team five points. Second place is worth three, and you get a single point for coming in third. Twice, I came in third.

Against Kennedy High, because some of my teammates couldn't make it, and because Kennedy didn't have much of a team, only three shot-putters, including me, were entered. So, even though my best throw was more than twenty feet behind the second-place dude, I got us a point. Check it. It's in the book. It was even in the paper: "3rd, Bennett, MSJ."

Another time, against the American Eagles, there were four of us competing. American had this one big, buff guy who kept fouling. Three times in a row, his foot was either on or over the line, so none of his mammoth throws counted. Officially, I beat him! As good as I felt, he must have felt really bad. His team-mates didn't cut him any slack. Half jokingly (but half seriously) they ripped into him. "Wait, that guy in the *wheelchair* beat you? How does that happen?" I just sat there, taking it all in, unable to mask my smile.

I'm never sure how to react when I get accolades and attention, especially when it's at the expense of my relatives, friends or, in one unforgettable case, a team-mate. Near the end of my senior year, I let loose with a fourteen-foot discus throw. Seeing how my previous best was barely eleven, I was stoked. So was my throwing coach, Mr. Moats, and so were my teammates. After the meet, they gathered around me. After Coach Moats announced my PR, a thunderous cheer erupted. Then, almost as an afterthought, he added that his son (and my teammate) Giancarlo also threw his personal best (which was about ten times farther than what I threw). There was only a smattering of polite applause.

Giancarlo, despite you shrugging it off and being sincerely happy for me that day (as was your dad), I still feel bad about it. I'm sorry, big guy!

Giancarlo: *Phil lived only a block away from me. We often traveled to school together. My father volunteered as our discus coach, so he also had a personal connection with Phil. I joined the track team my freshman year. At the beginning of our junior year, I had a talk with our head coach, Jack Marden, and his throwing coach, Ken Ferris, about possibly having Phil participate. Both were supportive. Phil joined the team and instantly became a cornerstone. At the start of each practice, following the team stretch, one lucky person got to lead the team in a warm-up lap around the track, pushing Phil the whole way. Doing so was considered an honor. Phil never missed a practice and usually stayed after the normal training to hit the weights with the rest of the throwers. At least until his doctor made him stop.*

Phil's stealing of the spotlight occurred multiple times, in both the discus and the shot put, and I never minded. His dedication put all of us to shame. It was really something to watch him tighten his safety belt, roll into the ring, lock his wheels, and heave a hunk of metal that weighed almost as much as he did.

Mom: *A kid in a wheelchair joining the track-and-field team is the ultimate oxymoron—except that is exactly what Phillip did. By his junior year in high school some of his close* *friends were in track. Somehow, they talked him into joining the throwers—the shot put and discus squad. Some people in wheelchairs have full upper-body strength. But Friedreich's ataxia attacks the arms just as much as the legs, so the odds of Phillip having any success throwing heavy objects were non-existent, but that didn't stop him. And it didn't stop the other members of the team from welcoming him and supporting him as he tried to acquire enough skill to just hold the shot or discus in his hand long enough to vaguely propel it in the right direction. Other throwers were sailing the discus 120 feet, while Phillip threw 11 feet. His shot sometimes didn't even make it over the stop board at the edge of the circle. But NEVER did anyone ever laugh.*

At one meet at American High School, there were only four competitors in the JV Shot category, of which Phillip was one. In each put Phillip managed to get the shot out of the circle, to a distance of four or five feet. His competitors were impressive. One of them, with the obvious physique of a shot-putter, heaved his shot with all his might—and fouled. The shot landed a great distance away, but outside the sector in which it must fall. Every time he tried harder, his shot went farther, but for some freaky reason it landed outside the desig-nated area. So each throw was disqualified and Phillip came in third, earning a point for Mission! I can only imagine the humiliation the losing athlete felt at having been beaten at his sport by a scrawny kid in a wheelchair whose arms barely worked.

Have you ever noticed that track athletes all know each other's personal record, or PR? They manage to keep track of each other's numbers and know when one of their team-mates has "PRed" (set a new personal record). If someone PRs during an event, it's not uncommon for fans and teammates to break out in spontaneous applause. At one major meet, Phillip's great friend, Giancarlo, PRed on his discus throw and received a polite ovation. Coincidentally, at the same meet, Phillip also PRed with a fourteen-foot discus throw. You should have heard the roar! The crowd went crazy. Even though Phillip's throw traveled only about 10 percent as far as Giancarlo's, the applause for Phillip was much, much louder. You would have thought he had just won Olympic gold. This time I felt bad for Phillip's teammate.

One of the parents there that day was Judge Squires, a California Superior Court judge who had two sons on the team. Phillip liked to brag that he performed in front of a judge. He had always been impressed by Judge Squires, yet at one of the last meets of Phillip's throwing career this proud, accomplished man said to Phillip "You're my hero." Phillip would never forget that.

Unfortunately, track couldn't last forever. At the year-end awards dinner, not only did I get my var-sity letter, but Coach Moats stood up and delivered a speech about me (which made my mom cry). Then, on behalf of the team, he gave me a commemorative discus, on which he had written with a big black marker: "PHIL 'BIG LOOGIE' BENNETT." The "Big Loogie" was a reference to my efforts to gather enough spit on my hands to better stick the discus to my palm so it wouldn't slip from my flimsy fingers. All season long, my teammates had joked about it, but it's now memorialized on the big-ass discus that sits on my bedroom shelf. When I see it, I view it not just as recognition for participating in a sport, but as a reward for reaching the stage of acceptance.

My most significant and memorable track-and-field moment had little to do with any actual throwing or even the relationships I built with my teammates. It was something that happened at my very last meet. It was held at James Logan High School in Union City. Lots of parents were there, including "the Judge"—Jeff and James Squires's dad, Judge Squires. Despite his super busy schedule, he managed to make it to many of our meets. The judge and I had spoken only a handful of times. I had always been rather intimidated by him. He was, after all, a judge. He even wore a distinguished-looking beard that confirmed his image as a wise man.

At the conclusion of that final meet, my track-and-field career now over, Judge Squires spoke the words that would change my attitude toward my disability forever. He said, "Phil, you're my hero."

Me? His hero? Seriously? Here's this incredibly successful and important person, and he's saying I'm *his* hero?

Later that night, after Mom helped me into my bed, I told her about what Judge Squires had said. I told her about how good and fortunate I felt. Throughout the years, so many people have gone out of their way to be nice to me.

Mom and I talked for a long time that night, and we realized something cool. My view of humanity is much more positive than most of my less disabled yet more cynical peers. My disability renders the goodness of humanity visible. My newfound awareness continues to manifest. Over and over, I see how my disability and vulnerability brings out people's best. I get to experience their goodness.

Two years later, while in college, I wrote about exactly that for Muscular Dystrophy Association's *Quest* magazine.

ꞇꜝ (ꞇꞃ, 2005)
The Upside of Disability" by Phil Bennett

Let's be honest: There aren't many positive aspects to living with a disability. I trip. I fall. Reality sucks. Life's miserable. Disability ruined my life and undermined my independence.

These pessimistic thoughts dominated my life for almost 11 years after I received a diagnosis of Friedreich's ataxia (FA) in 1994. But recently I've come to realize that these negative aspects distort the relatively few, but real, positive aspects to having a disability.

Disability has opened my eyes to the things that are usually overlooked by others — the selflessness and caring that people regularly demonstrate.

Signs of Caring

I attend a university with a massive campus and get around using a manual wheelchair. I must wheel from one corner of campus to another in 15 minutes, across streets and up elevators, praying that the professor is later than I am — all without an aide.

Complete strangers often offer a friendly push in the right direction, sometimes all the way to the front door of my classroom — even if it makes them tardy for their own engagements. As I roll toward the elevator, another student or sometimes even a professor may dart past me and press the elevator call button. Usually, they aren't even getting in themselves — they're going out of their way to save me time and effort. I never even have to ask.

California has very unpredictable weather, and once it began to rain immediately after a class. How was I going to get halfway across campus when rain was coming down in buckets, I didn't have a raincoat or umbrella, and there weren't any shelters?

A couple of students happened to be sprinting across the extensive courtyard huddled beneath a small umbrella clutched tightly against the wind. When they spotted me, they ran over and asked where I needed to go.

The husband immediately thrust his umbrella into my shaking wet hands and instructed me to hold it over both of our heads as he pushed me across the courtyard, up a ramp and into my building. After we caught our breath, we exchanged introductions, shook hands and went our separate ways — I to class, he back into the rain to find his abandoned wife.

Once I stopped to notice, I saw that my life was full of examples like these...The 12-year-old girl who, without any sign from me, stopped eating to open the heavy door of the pizza parlor. The homeless man who helped my dad carry me in my wheelchair up a long flight of stairs to catch a train.

Once, on an airplane, an abrupt knee spasm sent my food tray flying all over a big gruff motorcycle guy in the seat across the aisle. He never complained, never swore, never even sighed — just scooped off the sludge, called over the flight attendant and said, "Can we get another chicken dinner for this young man, please?"

Call it luck, coincidence or whatever you want. I call it goodness, a sign of caring, a sign of kindness.

Communication is Key

For a long time, I refused to think this way. I despised it when people treated me like a "helpless baby," asking if I needed help with rudimentary tasks. I *still* can't stand that paternalistic treatment, and I *still* get it every day!

But I've learned these encounters don't feel paternalistic when both parties approach the situation thoughtfully and respectfully. Helpers shouldn't be rude or patronizing, and — even if I don't *think* I need help — I need to be appreciative of their offers. They risked my frustration by offering assistance; the least I can do is give my gratitude in return.

It all depends on communication. Once a sophomore offered me a push to class. After I said I'd appreciate the help, *then* she admitted she "wasn't sure we're supposed to do this." She was willing to give me a push even before she knew if that would be a reasonable thing to do!

This helped me understand the monumental importance of good communication between people with and without disabilities. The goodness in humanity is always out there, but we need to use a degree of communication to tap it.

So I get a free push, saving me a few calories. But what do others get in return besides a tardy to class or a drenched body? Sure, I give them a nice smile and some words of appreciation, but they could get that at a Burger King.

Perhaps it's this: By being in a wheelchair, I exemplify the perseverance it takes to get up every morning, go to school, do homework and focus on the future. Maybe seeing my perseverance — and enabling it with their help — inspires people to persevere against the obstacles in their own lives.

In addition, my disability not only allows me to see the goodness in others, it encourages others to *act* upon their goodness.

The Downside of Normalcy

A disability renders visible the goodness of humanity. Sure, I want to walk again, I resent this disorder, I want to rid the world of it...but is its riddance worth being blind to this goodness?

In a way, this is almost a downside to normalcy: "Normal" people don't get to see the face of humanity that we folks with disabilities do.

I feel special and overjoyed when I get to an elevator and the button already has been pushed for me, or a stranger holds a door for me at the mall. That feeling yanks me out of the pit of despair that my disability puts me in, slaps me in the face, and makes me remember that people *do* care, that I still *am* loved, and that I'm *more* than my disability has made me.

So, here's the choice: Will you sulk about the disaster that a disability wreaks upon your life and dwell in the misery of its numerous negative aspects? Or will you recognize the positive aspects that it provides?

Choose wisely.

Others Like Us

As a matter of fact, I wrote several pieces for *Quest* magazine. (I was a journalism major, after all.) One of my favorite pieces was the one I wrote about the Muscular Dystrophy Association's summer camp. It was a place I could go and be surrounded by people a lot like me. It's something I've thought a lot about. Hanging out with your "own kind" gets a bad rap. Like you're racist or something. But it's not about that. There's just something special about finding others like us and being with them. Whether it's ethnicity, religion, age, sex, or having the same incurable disease, sometimes we need to be with people with whom we share a common experience. I love all kinds of people, but there's a distinct bond I can only forge with other FAers. That's what MDA Camp allowed me to do.

Quest (March/April, 2008): "MDA Summer Camp: Something for Everyone" by Phil Bennett

Every summer since 1955, kids have been granted the opportunity to escape the repetitious hardships of reality and relax among peers at one of MDA's summer camps, which now number more than 90. To make it even better, campers are able to attend at no cost to themselves or their families. The cost of camp is covered by generous donors all over the country, from individuals who bought an MDA Shamrock or made a Telethon donation, to large corporate sponsors.

At summer camp, rock 'n' roll takes on a whole new meaning.

I went to MDA summer camp for many years. Whenever my dad picked me up at week's end, he'd ask me how it was. I just said it was "great," before turning away and going to sleep (usually it had been a long night).

Here are some more thoughtful answers than mine as to the biggest highlights of this special week.

"The reasons I like MDA camp are: Seeing people that actually see you for who you are, being with people who are just like you, experiencing things you thought you could never do (i.e., horseback riding), and dancing without worrying if people are laughing at you," says Olivia Davis of Castro Valley, Calif., who was the MDA Goodwill Ambassador for Northern California in 2003. Olivia, 17, has congenital muscular dystrophy.

"MDA summer camp allows kids to have the childhood that many of us never are able to experience," says Laura-Beth Jacquin, 20, of Atlanta, Ga. The MDA Goodwill Ambassador for West Massachusetts in 2000, Laura-Beth has Friedreich's ataxia (FA). "I love to watch the other campers enjoy the relaxed, exciting and fun week of camp that everyone deserves to have."

"The people who go to camp are pretty much amazing," says Jennifer Sutton, 16, of McHenry, Ill., who also has FA. "They're like my second family — I've been going to camp for eight years and I've met my best friends there. I can be myself because I know everyone else is going through what I go through."

John Ryan, 19, of Spring Valley, N.Y., has FA. He says, "Every summer, I look forward to going to camp — it's definitely the highlight of the year for me. I look forward to seeing all my friends because camp is the only time when we can all hang out together. It's always so hard to say goodbye to all your friends, but we keep in touch and always look forward to next year."

"I would have to say it would definitely be people understanding having their toes run over," says Julie McMillian, 15, of Dacula, Ga., who has limb-girdle muscular dystrophy. "Since there are about 100 campers at MDA camp, counselors have gotten used to having their toes smashed." Julie also likes "meeting people with the same problems — it's nice to talk about your issues when someone is going through them, too. The counselors are the greatest people on Earth."

Apparently, this degree of respect is mirrored by MDA staff and volunteer counselors.

"The campers — seriously, they are so amazing!" says Amit Pande, a volunteer counselor from Berkeley, Calif.

Campers can try group activities they've never before experienced.

"MDA camp gave me new eyes to look at life with. I learned so much about what my real priorities are and how to make the best of every moment," says Brooke Falvey, a volunteer counselor from San Luis Obispo, Calif., adding, "Another great thing about camp is that not only do the younger children get a week to drag their feet and wheelchairs in the dirt without the constant nag of their parents, but their parents can have a relaxed state of mind knowing their children are having the time of their lives."

"In my opinion, the dances were the best part of MDA camp — all of the kids had a blast," said Stephanie Boyd, a volunteer counselor from Oakland,

Calif. "I'm not a great dancer, but you don't have to worry about being made fun of at MDA camp!"

"Everyone just lets loose and acts so very silly," says Leslie Uptain, MDA district director, San Francisco. "Where else can you find adults, counselors and staff dressed like 80s rock stars throwing water balloons at each other in a fit of giggles?"

"I love my son and, believe me, taking care of him and meeting his challenges is one of the most wonderful things in my life," says Debbie Walker, of Powder Springs, Ga., referring to 13-year-old Jake, who has type 2 spinal muscular atrophy. "However, it's really nice to know that once a year my husband and I can 'escape' the day-to-day grind and have an opportunity to relax and simply focus on ourselves and each other. We generally plan a getaway and enjoy the time that he's at camp."

Christopher Johnson, 16, of Marietta, Ga., has Duchenne muscular dystrophy. He loves camp because "you get to interact socially with people just like you without being looked upon as different."

Adds his mother, Cheryl, "Knowing that he's well taken care of and happy, I can take a break from care taking and recharge."

So the verdict seems pretty unanimous — MDA summer camp really is a bit more than fun in the sun for campers, counselors and parents alike.

ᚠᚠᚠ ᚠᚠᚠ—ᚠᚠ ᚠᚠᚠ
Rock Bottom—and Back

There's no shortage of metaphors that depict life's ups and downs: Roller coasters. The stock market. Cloudy and sunny days. Mountain peaks and valleys…Despite the FA, I've had my share of ups. But I'd be lying if I said I didn't get serious cases of the blues. For obvious reasons, they're cases that are probably way worse than most people get.

If you ask me what the worst moment of my life has been, I can instantly zero in on it. It wasn't the time when some friends carried me downstairs so recklessly (while I was in my wheelchair) that I feared for my life. It wasn't the time when some screw-up airline employee broke my wheelchair, stranding me at the airport for hours. It wasn't the time I sat in the cold and rain waiting for a tardy Paratransit bus while desperately busting for a pee. It wasn't the time when I stumbled and fell onto the bathroom floor in my dad's house, splitting open the front of my head. It wasn't even the times—way too many of them!—when I was rejected by the girls on match.com.

No, it was the spinal fusion surgery I underwent on January 10, 2001. I was sixteen years old when they plastered that damn cast around my chest and back. I'll never forget the pain. Still, the truth is, I'm actually glad that I had the surgery. Even knowing what I know now, I would suffer through it again.

Scoliosis (a curvature of the spine) is one of the grab bag of nasty side effects of Friedreich's ataxia. Almost everyone with FA develops scoliosis, and almost all of us need spinal fusions to prevent it from getting so bad that if affects our heart's capacity to pump and our lungs' ability to breathe. My orthopedist had been monitoring my developing scoliosis since I was first diagnosed in 1994. Five years later, in the fall of '99, he broke the inevitable news. My time had come. He referred me to a specialist, Dr. James Shively, a pediatric orthopedic surgeon with experience in high-risk patients like me.

At first, I was not on board. But the consultation with Dr. Shively went better than I thought it would. By the time I left his office, I felt better. Also, so I could join a Make-A-Wish trip to meet Arnold Schwarzenegger and go on a Christmas cruise with my family, he agreed to postpone the surgery until January, immediately after my first semester finals.

We had to be at Oakland Children's Hospital at some crazy predawn hour. Supposedly, the surgery would take several hours! I can't tell you anything about the procedure because I was in la-la land. But here's what I learned afterward:

What Dr. Shively and his assistant, Dr. Burnham, did during all those hours was pretty damn amazing. They sliced open my back from my neck to just below my waist. They removed all the discs from between the vertebrae (that's T4 to L4 if you're up on your human anatomy), and then they packed the spaces where the discs used to reside with donor bone grafts. (Whenever I'm not myself, it's because I have parts of others inside me, damn it!) Titanium rods were inserted on the sides of my spine, running from top to bottom. Both were attached at the top with clamps and anchored at the bottom with two screws that were drilled directly into the large lumbar vertebrae. Like little metal wings, the rods were wired to each vertebra. I know this because I have seen the x-rays of my spine. The hardware is clearly visible. I have no idea how they managed to do all that without damaging my spinal cord. By the time Dr. Shively and Dr. Burnham were finished, my curve had been reduced from forty-five to ten degrees.

After it was over, my mom and dad had to wait a long time before they could come into the recovery room. They told me that I looked absolutely awful—that the only way they knew that I was alive was the heart monitor's steady, reassuring beep. Apparently, I was ghastly gray and so cold that they were pumping warm air under the covers in an attempt to raise my body temperature.

Right about then, you'd think the worst was over, right? But it wasn't. Not by a long shot. Once I was out of recovery, they wheeled me into the intensive care unit (ICU). Mom and/or Dad were always there. At night they'd take turns sleeping on the folding chair beside my bed. It was a good thing, too, because I was totally out of it and couldn't communicate with the staff.

I was hooked up to a morphine drip, that, theoretically, I could self-administer with the push of a button. No one but me was supposed to push it. Well, that only works if you *can* push the button. But between my Friedreich's ataxia and the knock-you-out drugs flowing through my body, there was no way I could push it! So, when I needed a hit of morphine, my parents would put my thumb on the button, place theirs on top of it and push.

The day following my surgery I got a roommate—a young girl who had just undergone the same surgery I had had, performed by the same two surgeons. Unlike me, she didn't have Friedreich's ataxia and she wasn't in a wheelchair. Not everyone who has scoliosis surgery is in a wheelchair. In fact, the vast majority of scoliosis patients are otherwise healthy. They walk in and walk out. The hospital staff members are used to these "typical" scoliosis patients.

So, perhaps it was understandable when, the day after my surgery, the nurses and nurse's assistants planned to get me up on my feet. After all, this usually speeds up recovery. So, they gave me a muscle relaxant (which made me virtually unconscious for twenty-four hours) and then tried to get me to stand up. They had no clue how dangerous this was, and if my parents hadn't been there to bellow "STOP!" the nurse would have attempted to force me to my feet. If she had, I would have crumpled to the floor, and I dread to think what damage would have been done to my fancy new hardware. Fortunately, thanks to my parents' quick thinking—*and them being there*—we averted that catastrophe.

On the morning of "day three," they released me from the ICU and put me into a regular hospital room. Sounds like things must have been finally looking up by then, right? But, no, I still hadn't experienced the most horrible part of the nightmare. That afternoon, I was scheduled to be casted. They needed to keep me rigid while all the new bone healed, so I needed an armpits-to-hips cast.

While friends and family waited for me in my room, Dad accompanied me to what I'll forever refer to as "the casting." I had no idea what I was in for.

Dad: *I think I shut out most of that process. It was awful and excruciatingly painful for Phil to go through. The "cast tech" really seemed to have a hard time with the process. The* *apparatus used to prepare Phil for casting was a Heath Robinson-looking contraption…Frankensteinian! The part over his spine supported him while he was rotated, kind of like a rotisserie. Throughout the procedure, my son screamed with pain. It really shook me up watching him suffer so. They put something over his spine during the casting and then, once the cast was set, they had to pull it out. He had to be x-rayed, so his mom and I wheeled him down to x-ray where he had to sit in front of the x-ray machine while we propped him up. Then the dumb aide who wheeled his IV alongside us walked off to the side without warning and almost tore the needle out of his arm. I headed home afterward, crying most of the way. I stopped at Trader Joe's and bought a bottle of whiskey. I reached the house with bloodshot eyes, which had nothing to do with the unopened whiskey. It's terrible to watch your child suffer when there is so little you can do about it. I endured this for sixteen years.*

Meanwhile Mom and my visitors were waiting for me to return to my room. When I finally got there, I felt so horrible that I asked them all to leave. As if to prove how bad I felt, I threw up.

Now *that* was the worst experience of my life.

It didn't quickly or magically heal. I was in so much pain that I wasn't interested in eating or drinking. I just shut down. More than a bit desperate, Mom and Dad took a bold step and checked me out ahead of schedule. They figured they had already learned what they needed to know about my post-op care. At the hospital, they learned how to use a sheet to roll me like a log. Moving my back even a little bit was excruciatingly painful. So, we brought home an egg-crate foam mattress pad and lots of little pillows to pack around me.

Mom: *At the hospital, we were really worried about him. He wasn't engaged at all; his eyes had a glazed look. We hoped that being back home would perk him up and help him snap out of his daze. It actually worked—and quite quickly. Here's why:*

Phillip's church group had been scheduled to visit him in the hospital on Sunday—six days after his surgery—but we decided to take him home on Saturday.

So, instead, the group visited our home. We roused Phillip from his bed and helped him recline on his La-Z-Boy. Happily, the visit made a huge, helpful difference. Because he wanted to engage with his friends, Phillip talked, smiled, joked, and laughed. It was a momentous turning point. Human contact had a magical effect. One day Phillip was sitting in his recliner, but he was in a lot of pain. He insisted that he would be more comfortable if he could lie flat on the floor. So that's where we put him—right smack in the middle of our carpeted family room. He lay there for a while, still feeling quite miserable, when his old buddy, Travis Silva, surprised him with a visit. Phillip, who had dozed off, awoke to Travis's grinning mug and returned the smile. Although he was still hurting, the two talked, sharing stories. *Travis's visit definitely perked up Phillip's spirits.*

Travis Silva: *There were a few times when Phil was laid up for whichever reason, so I'd visit him. On his back in the living room rings a vague bell, but the visit that most stands out in my mind happened during our first year of college. I had gone away to school, and Phil had stayed in Fremont. I went to Phil's house just to hang out for a bit. Valerie had a slightly different plan for me, though. Maybe she had an errand to run or maybe Phil was just hankering to get out of the house. When I got to the door, she handed me the keys to their van and told me I was taking Phil to lunch.*

I had known Valerie since I was five, and even at nineteen or twenty she very much remained a mom figure, so I wasn't about to argue. Still, I was somewhat surprised that she wanted me to drive the van, but she knew my grandfather is a paraplegic and owned a similar van, so maybe that played into her thinking. At any rate, we drove to a local deli that Phil liked and had lunch. I remember having a good conversation. Phil was funny and fun and charming as always. But I also remember that I had to help him cut his food. I'd known him since kindergarten, and I had seen the long arc of his symptoms, including when he started using his chair in eighth grade. Yet, watching him struggle to eat that day was sobering. How Phil could overcome that challenge while maintaining his incredible sense of humor is nothing short of miraculous.

Mom: *That post-surgery month was a tough one. Phillip was hurting. Moving him even slightly would hurt him more. It was such hard work! Each morning, just to lift Phillip from his bed into his recliner, his dad would drive all the way from his house in Pleasanton to my house in Fremont. Then, each evening, he would do it again so he could put him back into his bed. Each night, Phillip would wake up several times, needing repositioning. I was a wreck. Thankfully, my parents stayed with us for a whole month. They were a tremendous help. I don't think I could have made it through the ordeal without them.*

Dad: *On top of everything else, Phil had severe constipation, caused by the meds. It was days before he could go to the bathroom. He strained so much his nose bled.*

Three weeks after the surgery, I felt like I needed to get my butt back to school, but that wasn't going to happen. So the school sent two teachers to my house. Originally, they had planned three months of this at-home instruction, but after about six weeks of it, I'd had enough. I was so sick of being stuck at home that I asked—more like demanded—that I be allowed to go back to school. (If, five years earlier, you had told me that, someday, I'd be yearning for school, I would have insisted that you were nuts!) I could barely lift my arms, but I needed to get back to my friends. Being around them has always been my favorite part of school anyway. So the school district sprung the necessary cash to provide me with an aide. I can't even remember the first one's name. It's just as well because she was useless. She told me I should be pushing my own (manual) wheelchair—that she shouldn't be doing it for me. Which would have been a good idea except for one minor detail—it was impossible! I just wasn't strong enough yet to do that. After I told my mom what she said, it wasn't long before I got a new, improved aide.

That cast stayed on for three months. I still had it on in late March when my mom and I ventured to Biloxi, Mississippi, to the National Ataxia Foundation's annual conference. Finally, after what seemed like forever, a nurse cut it off, freeing me. Because it had a lot of cool autographs and comments on it, my mom wanted to save it. She stored it in my closet. Still, I hated it so much that, eventually, I talked her into getting rid of it. I didn't want it around anymore. Too many painful (literally) memories.

So why on earth would I say that I'm glad I had the surgery and that I'd agree to go through that hell again? Simple. The upside has been fantastic. Most obvious is that it did exactly what it was supposed to do. Ten years later my spine is still straight, my heart and lungs have not been crushed by a curved and twisted spine, and I don't have the terrible back pain that many FAers experience. There was an unexpected upside, too. Not long after I returned to school and had built up some strength, people treated me differently. They weren't afraid to touch me. One of my teachers would even give me a friendly smack on the back to accompany his hello. He would never have done that B.S. (before surgery). B.S., people had been afraid I'd break, and no wonder. If you look at my before pictures, you see me all slumped over, but now, afterward, I sit up straight. Sure, my new look may just be an outward appearance, but the surgery did make me look stronger, healthier, and more grown up. Enduring spinal cord surgery was a classic example of postponing immediate gratification (in this case, avoiding pain!) for a long-term reward.

Had I still been all hunched over, I doubt Dane and Giancarlo would have pushed me to join the shot put and discus squad. If my friends thought I was brittle, I doubt they would have been so quick to hoist me and my chair over obstacles. With my newly gained three inches in height, I could make better eye contact and engage with people more. In many ways, large and small, the worst time of my life improved my life.

ᴡᴀᴋᴍᴀᴄ ᴊᴍᴃᴃᴊᴍᴄ

M a k i n g   a   D i f f e r e n c e

Ivy Wu, one of the Fremont Unified School District's board members, says:

"We aren't who *we* think we are. We aren't who *others* think we are. We are who *we think others think* we are."

It's a little confusing. But when you think about it, it makes sense. We are who we think others think we are. One thing I think others think *I* am is inspiring. Oops, that makes me sound conceited. Still, if I had a dollar for every time someone said, "Phil, you're so inspiring!" I'd be a wealthy guy.

If I am inspiring, I want it to be because of how I live. To say that I've had to overcome obstacles would be, in my biased opinion, the understatement of the century (even if it is early in the century). I know a lot of people are paying attention to how I'm playing the pathetically poor hand I've been dealt. That's why I try to be positive. That's why I joke around and have fun.

That's a big reason why I do all the crazy stuff I do—to show everyone I can that no matter the circumstances, you've got to live. Fully and completely live.

I want it to be more than that, though. I want to do something concrete. Something measurable. With that objective in mind, I began doing all I could to raise money to fund a cure for Friedreich's ataxia. As of now, thanks to four successful events, we've raised a little over two hundred thousand dollars.

My fund-raising goals began soon after my mom and I returned from the 2001 National Ataxia Foundation's annual meeting, held that year in frigid Minnesota. Whenever we attended FA conferences, Mom and I went our separate ways. At the Minneapolis one, a cool teen program had been organized, and I was still mobile enough to get around in my wheelchair without help.

While I was hanging out with the other kids at the pool and hot tub or eating pizza in the teen room, my mom was listening to lectures from the various doctors, hoping to learn about the latest research. As she would say, "Those were heady days." The FA gene had been first discovered in 1996. In just five years it seemed like researchers had learned so much and had come surprisingly and encouragingly far. Mom was so optimistic about a cure being found that it was hard not to catch her confidence.

Still, why does everything have to be about money? Should whether we find a cure for a disease—FA, cancer, diabetes, or anything else—depend upon cash? It just doesn't seem right. But that's our reality.

Anyway, one of the studies Mom learned about at that 2001 conference was one that had just been funded. A couple of scientists got to spend six months figuring out if some theory they had would actually stand up to testing. I don't remember anything about that particular study, probably because nothing came of it. But I do remember that the grant was for twenty-five thousand dollars.

Mom had spent all four days of the conference with Bruce and Cindy Olson. The Olsons had two children with FA. They were also the local National Ataxia Foundation (NAF) chapter organizers and had thrown several gala dinner fund-raisers, one of which had raised twenty thousand dollars! At first, Mom and I thought that seemed unbelievable and unachievable. Then, after we talked about it, we thought maybe it wasn't a pipe dream. Maybe it wasn't an unattainable goal. If a research grant was twenty-five thousand dollars, and a single fund-raiser could raise twenty thousand dollars, then not only could we do it, we *had* to do it.

We felt empowered. Instead of sitting around hoping for a miracle, we could organize fund-raisers that could directly lead to finding a cure for Friedreich's ataxia. From that moment on, I had a purpose. The bit was between my teeth, and I've refused to let it go.

Besides raising money, fund-raising has allowed me to discover how compassionate, selfless, and helpful some people can be. Mom and I began recruiting people to be part of our organizing committee. Thankfully, several stepped forward. Paul Konanz, Brianne's dad, had an obvious personal connection with our cause, so he immediately became a huge contributor. My gran and granddad flew down from Edmonton, Alberta, Canada, just to help. But it's not only those with a link to FA that support us. Others, only because they know me, have adopted our cause and helped us tremendously. James Leeper and his wife, Sharon Cooper, once my parents' business associates and now extremely close family friends, not only talked the owners of the Rosenblum Cellars Winery (in nearby Alameda) into letting us have dinner dances there, they somehow convinced Kent and Kathy Rosenblum to donate all the wine! That was huge.

As it is with most things, our first fund-raising event was the hardest. But it was also the most exciting. We began by seeking help from the pros at the local Muscular Dystrophy Association office. Because we had attended so many fund-raisers, we knew many of the MDA professionals. We hoped to learn from their expertise.

One lesson they taught us was that the road to fund-raising success would be loaded with land mines, the first and most obvious being finding a venue.

Immediately, we got lucky. Dr. and Mrs. Taghioff (that cool guy who diagnosed me for free) had bought our house and land after Mom and Dad split up. On our former property, he built a crazy luxurious mansion with a gorgeous view of San Francisco Bay and a deck engineered to hold 350 people. (I know this because he never stops reminding us of it!) Dr. and Mrs. Taghioff were beyond generous, and I'll never forget their kindness. They allowed us to host our first event, Sunset on Friedreich's Ataxia, at their amazing home.

Another family of angels that came through for us was the Balch family. When we lived next door to them, Jack and Patti Balch were the perfect neighbors. Whenever we had to search for our roving German shorthaired pointer, Heidi, they let us freely wander about their property calling her name. Frequently, we'd find Heidi warming herself by their fireplace. When Heidi was on her last legs, one final time she dragged herself over to their front porch. The Balches let her in, covered her with a blanket, and comforted her as she breathed her final breaths. Great folks. They volunteered to be our "presenting sponsors." (That's a fancy way of saying they wrote us a ten-thousand-dollar check!)

Our fund-raisers expanded my circle of relationships and friendships. I got to know Sam Van Zandt. My mom knew who he was because he was a popular DJ on a San Francisco oldies radio station. Even though, now and then, I'll listen to a light rock station, I wasn't much into oldies back then. Sam had also been the voice of the television show *Candid Camera*, so he was kind of a celebrity. His *three* sisters had Friedreich's ataxia, so he was personally acquainted with its horrors. Sam volunteered to be our master of ceremonies—our official "famous person." Not only was he an excellent emcee, he became a good friend. He even invited me to his radio station for an in-studio interview just so I could promote our fund-raiser. (A fringe benefit was getting a close-up look at the behind the scenes and inner workings of a radio station.) At all four of our fund-raisers, Sam was at the helm, leading us like the pro he is.

The goal for our first Sunset on Friedreich's Ataxia was twenty-five thousand dollars. To be honest, even though a lot of people dug deep and worked hard— even on the night after the event, the committee members were up until past 2:00 a.m.—I wasn't sure we could do it. But guess what? We ended up clearing almost fifty thousand dollars. It was such a fantastic feeling—I felt like it was all for me, personally, and I suppose it was. I mean, the fund-raising pros say people give to people, not causes.

I was hooked. Hooked on the possibility that I could do something that would lead to a cure for this horrible disorder. Hooked on throwing incredibly grand parties. Hooked on donning my tuxedo and being the center of attention. (Yes, I'll admit it.) Hooked on all the hugs, laughs, and dances I could get in one evening. All of it was addicting.

Stoked by success, we began to plan the next event. Each time, they got better and better. Rosenblum Winery in Alameda became our home venue, and Outback Steakhouse became our home restaurant. Astonishingly, they fed everyone for free. All attendees got a steak dinner.

How does this happen? Well, one piece of advice I feel qualified to offer you is this: Get to know people. Don't collect coins, stamps, or baseball cards. Collect people! Relationships are everything. For example, I got to know Mr. Pat Kruk, part owner and manager of a bunch of Bay Area Outback Steakhouses. Pat and his staff sponsored the annual Ruby Hill Celebrity Golf Tournament (held annually in Livermore, California, at the Ruby Hill Golf Club) to benefit the Muscular Dystrophy Association. Remember, Friedreich's ataxia is a form of MD. So, because I was one of "Jerry's Kids," I was a Ruby Hill regular.

I'd spend the day out on the golf course, often getting seriously sunburned. After turning twenty-one, I'd also get seriously sloshed. Rich people would pay to come and spend the day golfing with famous sports personalities. I got to meet John Madden, Jim Plunkett, and several of the San Jose Earthquakes. Outback Steakhouse would feed them all day, starting with a breakfast that included "eye-opener" beverages. Later, on the course, there'd be a big burger lunch. Then, after the golfing, inside the club, a gourmet dinner would be served. While they dined, players were entertained (or, maybe, bored) by speeches and award presentations.

A couple of times I was one of the dinner speakers. I would thank the golfers for coming and for raising a bundle of money for MDA. Mr. Kruk must have been impressed, because when the time came to put on our own events at the Rosenblum Cellars, he stepped forward and offered to feed our crowd, too. His staff (most of whom were about my age) volunteered their time—on a Saturday evening, no less. The food was scrumptious. Another time, Mr. Kruk let us host a fund-raiser luncheon at the Outback in Fremont. It raised four thousand bucks. His kindness and generosity really blew me away. Still does. I am fortunate to have him in my life.

The truth is, lots of people have been beyond generous with their time and money to…well…to save my life. My friend Travis Silva's mom, who, in addition to being a lifelong supporter (I've known Travis since kindergarten), owns Vintage Catering. Charging us zero, Mrs. Silva catered the desserts at many of our fund-raisers. Friends and friends of friends have donated auction items as glamorous as a week at a condo in Hawaii. Because of people like these, we've raised that two hundred thousand dollars, every penny of it going to Friedreich's ataxia research. My mom and I are extremely picky about where all the cash goes. We keep track of which researchers receive the dollars we raise, and we closely follow their work.

Sadly, since 2007 we haven't planned a major fund-raising event. My mom says she's dropped the ball, that it's too much work, and she doesn't have the time to put another event together. It's not just her, though. I need to push harder and not rely only on her. Trust me. I haven't given up. I'm still hoping we can come up with something new. Friedreich's ataxia hasn't been cured yet. Until it is, I'm going to keep striving to drum up every dollar I can so the research can continue.

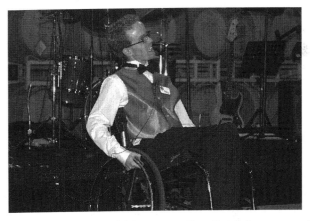

Phillip making one of his many fund-raising speeches.

The FAmily Effect

Perhaps no one has been affected more by my life more than my little brother, Brian. Not in a good way, either. Oh, we love each other alright, and I've never done anything to hurt him—intentionally, at least. But hurt him I have.

Look, I get it. I understand both sides. I understand that my parents felt they had to do everything they could to help me, and that my needs have always been super time-consuming. Time is finite, and every minute spent with me at the doctor, at a conference, on an outing—daily or weekly—or simply helping me get geared up to go anywhere has been a minute spent away from Brian. So, I understand why he has always felt shortchanged. I don't fault my parents for anything they have done for me, but I definitely don't blame Brian for feeling mistreated, ignored, or abandoned. When the devastating effects of Friedreich's ataxia are listed, the focus is on how it affects the patient. But FA is lethal in other ways. What it does to families (certainly what it did to mine) can be equally devastating.

Brian: *I always looked up to Phil. He has always been smart as hell. I have nothing against him whatsoever. When we were kids, not only was he my big brother, he was my closest friend, my babysitter, and my playmate. Phil was excellent at strategy games and a master of video games, especially Super Nintendo 64 and the Legend of Zelda. For that and because he looked after me and treated me well, I admired Phil—a lot. When I was having problems with our dad, I depended on him for guidance and protection, and he was always there. Phil took care of me.*

Still, I always thought my parents loved Phil more than they loved me. He got all the attention. Sometimes I wondered if they even knew (or even cared) if I was alive. Now that I'm grown and more mature, I know that I share a lot of the blame. I don't think I was born to be bad, but I was a bad kid. Would I have been better if Phil had been born healthy? Would I have had fewer problems if I had received more attention? Probably.

My parents met in Europe. My dad operated a bus tour business in England. My mom was a passenger, touring the UK as part of the University of Alberta's concert choir. It didn't take long for them to connect. Before Phil was born, though, they were having problems. There was a lot of yelling in our house. I'm often asked if Phillip's condition led to my parents' divorce. My answer is that it contributed to it, but it didn't cause it. If he had been born without FA, I think they still would have split up. With or without us, they just weren't a good match. As far as I can tell, their marriage was over before Phil's diagnosis—but his diagnosis speeded things up.

Because of the massive attention paid to Phil—everyone loved him—it felt like I didn't exist. So I guess it's no surprise that when I was twelve and in sixth grade, I began seriously messing up. The main reason was that I wanted a family. Since I didn't feel like I had one at home, I went looking for one outside it.

I found one, sort of, with the wrong crowd. Whereas Phil's friends were stellar kids, mine were always in trouble. Phil's friends and my friends didn't get along. I plugged myself in with the gang bangers and druggies. By seventh grade, I was smoking pot. Drugs were my escape. I did it to gain acceptance. I didn't care about school. I was a terrible student. I wouldn't listen to anyone. I didn't do my homework. I didn't study. I wouldn't even try. I got kicked out of high school and moved in with my dad who, after the divorce, had moved to nearby Pleasanton. Then I got kicked out of school there, too. Today, if I were my father, I'd beat my own ass!

Phil played more sports in high school than I did. He was what I call an exploratory guy. He wanted to do and try everything. Even after he was stuck in a wheelchair, he was doing all sorts of wild stuff—skiing, skydiving, river rafting, hell, he even went to a biker camp. Phil was a badass, but a cool, lovable one. He did more than I ever did or will. While Phil was doing everything, I lived in a bubble. A bad bubble.

By the time I turned fifteen, I felt like I was raising myself. Mom was always off with Phil somewhere, and Dad was either working or with Phil, too. Again, I don't blame them. They did what they had to do, but the lack of attention deeply affected me. They would spend three thousand dollars on a wheelchair, so obviously there wasn't much left over for anything I'd want. But it wasn't about money. It was about time. There wasn't enough of it spent on me.

Dad couldn't deal with what Phil was going through. Who could? He was a drinker, too. I don't blame him. Phil's condition was devastating. I was a kid and didn't fully understand. But my dad? He knew what Phil was up against.

Dad remarried, but my stepmom couldn't (or wouldn't) ever accept Phil's condition. When he'd come stay with us on weekends, it was uncomfortable. Eventually, they divorced and it was probably a good thing. Sometimes divorce is better for the kids than staying together and battling it out over issues that will never be resolved—like Phil's ataxia.

After getting kicked out of my second high school—for smoking pot on campus—I was assigned 150 hours of community service and 150 hours of drug rehabilitation. I had to go to court and fight to get back into school. I was successful and ultimately graduated, but I was not allowed to participate in the graduation ceremony. I was far from rehabbed, though. I was still buying, selling, and using drugs. I got into a fistfight with my dad. I lived in a Volkswagen for a month. A friend offered me a job in Reno, but I fell in with the wrong crowd there, too. Everything that happened in Reno was bad.

I moved back to the Bay Area and eventually, somehow, I got it together. I'm still not sure exactly how. I was tired of being in trouble. I matured. I met the right girl, and I know that love had a lot to do with it. It definitely helps to have loving parents. Despite everything, I never doubted that they loved me. I've made amends with my dad. Now, I work for him, manufacturing and installing cabinetry. And my mom? Oh my gosh! My mom is like God's fingertip. I swear, she's an angel. What she's done for Phil has been unimaginably selfless and heroic. Her love knows no bounds. Just like she refused to give up on him, she refused to give up on me. Today I'm married, responsible, and clean.

I don't know if it's possible to effectively parent in a situation like ours—a first child cursed with a crippling disease and a second child blessed with good health. My parents were caught off guard. They had no guidance on how to play the hand they were dealt. Hell, raising a "normal," healthy child is a major challenge, and Mom and Dad had to deal with both of us. Under the circumstances, they did the best they could.

Which was another motivation and purpose for me to write this book. Perhaps if parents with special-needs children use my story as a cautionary tale, what happened to Brian won't happen to the siblings of other kids with serious health issues. In Fremont, where I live, there's an organization called Friends of Children with Special Needs (FCSN). Its mission is to "help individuals with special needs and their families find love, hope, respect, and support through integrated community involvement." One of the things they're really into is attending to the needs of the too-often-neglected brothers and sisters of special-needs children. If FCSN had been around when I was a kid, if my parents had known about it, who knows? Maybe many of Brian's travails could have been circumvented. So, if you're a parent reading this, as much as kids like me desperately need you, so do their brothers and sisters.

Don't forget about them.

Dad: *When I first heard the terrible term "Friedreich's ataxia," Valerie and I had already been sleeping in separate rooms—things were not good in our relationship. So, no, it wasn't Phillip's condition that caused our separation and ultimately our divorce. But it didn't help matters much, either.*

My sons were challenging in different ways. Phillip's physical limitations were offset by the fact that he was curious, bright, and compliant. He was the academic child. Brian was healthy and athletic, but not studious and was drawn to the less-desirable kids in school. How much of that was Brian and how much was the atmosphere he grew up in is hard to say. Brian is very much like his dad. I see a lot of me in him.

Brian is sensitive. He feels that his brother always got the premier attention. That's partly true. It had to be. But I did coach him in soccer for twelve years. I coached Phillip for a few years, too, before it became apparent that soccer wasn't his bag. Some years I coached both kids' teams. Watching Brian run was a beautiful sight. I wish he had chosen track over pot. He loves fishing. Show him any kind of fishing hole and he will find a string, rig a hook, and chase shadows all day long. I hope he appreciates what a great person he is. Brian has so many skills and talents.

As the years went by, PJ required more and more support. Brian was off doing his thing mostly. Valerie and I had our schedules intertwined to provide 24-7 coverage. We were always available to the other in case there was a crisis. Cell phones were essential to our lifestyles. Now, I hate the things. The point is, there were just not enough hours in the day to take care of all of Phillip's needs and all of Brian's, too. But we tried. We tried hard.

My approach to Phillip's illness was different than his mother's. Valerie is religious. I am not. I felt that she adopted an unrealistic and overly rosy view of Phil's future. For a long time she was convinced a cure was around the corner. However, she and Phil worked very hard at fundraising for the cure. I believe she will stay involved in the Friedreich's Ataxia Research Alliance. I probably will not.

I focused on Phil's practical issues—modifying his wheel-chair, making sure he had a working cell phone and electric toothbrushes, finding condom catheters, etc. I built ramps at both houses and worked hard to ensure that he had good wheelchair access at his high school and at San Jose State. And, of course, I spent hours and hours just talking with him about stuff.

Both Valerie and I did everything we could for Phil. It still does not feel like enough. But our approaches were totally different.

Valerie and I are now bound in deep mutual understanding of extraordinary grief. It supplants any periodic animosity that we have/had toward each other. Even the people now closest to us have no idea. We both carry an immense pain that neither of us expects to ever go away. It is a very personal pain. Brian will have some of that, too.

When Brian was in eighth grade, he came to live with me full-time. When he was young, he did reasonably well in school and was manageable. Once his hormones kicked in, however, he was difficult to control. He and I had constant conflicts. He stole from me. Before he had his driver's license, he "borrowed" my car without asking and took it for a spin. He took my girlfriend's BMW on a joyride. He smashed a kitchen chair over the counter. We got to know every cop in Pleasanton. He'd disappear. Or he'd tell me he was at a friend's house. When I'd call the parents to see if he was really there, a lot of times he wouldn't be. I frequently searched his room for contraband and even resorted to removing his bedroom door. I took classes on how to raise a difficult teenager.

I always told him I loved him, though, and today, miraculously, we get along great.

Mom: *I think Brian is correct in his assessment that Phillip's diagnosis didn't—by itself—cause Tim's and my divorce. However, it was more than our marriage could handle. Looking back, I think it's a shame we couldn't have stayed together, because neither of us is a horrible person. For Phillip's sake, it would have been better if we had stayed together.*

There was some good that came out of our splitting up, though. As Phillip became older, and the FA progressed, taking care of him became an increasingly weighty responsibility. It was incredibly hard work. When Phillip was at the other parent's house, we could have some private and desperately needed personal time.

I once told Phillip that, although he was afflicted with Friedreich's ataxia, he was not the only one affected by it. And though his father and I have been affected in countless ways, the person most profoundly changed other than Phillip himself would have to be his brother, Brian.

Brian was born in the shadow of his luminescent older brother. They had a very good relationship, because Phillip loved everyone and everyone loved Phillip, including his little brother. They were each other's primary playmate. As Brian grew closer to Phillip in size (if not age) and as Phillip's physical capabilities began to wane (before we knew why), they were a well-matched pair for several years.

But Phillip's intellectual and social brilliance made Brian's excellent brain and wit seem pale in comparison—to no one more than Brian himself. And even when Brian's natural physical aptitude allowed him to clearly excel over his brother, it was in the new shadow of the decline of Phillip's physical abilities. How could Brian celebrate his soccer prowess fully when Phillip could no longer play soccer at all? What fun could riding his bike be when Phillip could no longer ride a bike?

The day I came home from the doctor with Phillip's diagnosis was the day any hope of Brian having a normal childhood was dashed. The affect the diagnosis had on his father and I changed the way we responded to everything—including Brian. Initially our lives revolved around Phillip because of the grief, and the revolving door of doctors' appointments. That initial phase where our lives stood still was for about six months. I have tried to imagine what that was like for Brian as a seven-year-old, watching his life change around him with no real understanding of why. He couldn't see anything different about Phillip. But suddenly life revolved around Phillip.

Then, at the tender age of nine, Brian's parents split up and his life was shoved further asunder. The house that Brian *absolutely loved, with five acres for him to explore, was sold, and each of his parents set up a new household. As divorces go, ours was reasonably civilized. Phillip's condition kept things in perspective. But very soon Brian found himself carrying a much greater burden of responsibility than any nine-year-old should. Because I was a single mom, Brian became my other pair of hands. Whether it was moving furniture around or helping with Phillip, I depended on him to help me. By the time Brian was eleven, Phillip had transitioned into the wheelchair. Everywhere we went involved transferring Phillip into the front seat, then loading his wheelchair into the back of the station wagon. I wonder how many times Brian loaded that chair into the back of that car! Whenever I traveled with Brian and Phillip, Brian was my navigator and partner. When the three of us were flying home from Hawaii, I'll never forget the look on Brian's face when I dropped him, Phillip, and our luggage at the terminal then left them there while I returned the rental car. There he was, just twelve years old, left to be responsible for his older, wheelchair-bound brother and all our baggage.*

The weight of his responsibility forced Brian to grow strong and confident. He was way ahead of his peers—mature beyond his years. Today, as a young adult, the contrast with others his age is clear. And while the boot camp of those years helped build the strong, confident Brian that I am proud of, as his mother I wish he had been spared the experience and he could have been a child a bit longer.

Children believe their mother's kiss can heal any wound, and their father's hands can repair anything that breaks. As they move toward adulthood, they naturally believe that they are invincible—it's a normal part of their developing psyche. But Phillip's diagnosis shattered Brian's confidence in life. His mother and father—even the doctors—couldn't make his brother better. And if his brother could get sick and die, then life was not something you could trust. This loss of faith in the order of the universe has been the most significant effect Friedreich's ataxia has had on Brian.

Brian's loss of faith played out through his teen years in some pretty obstructive and destructive behavior. What's the point in working hard to get good grades? What's the point in planning for a future? If life can let you down this badly, why not push the boundaries to see just how invincible you really are? Why worry about repercussions? Why not live for today, because tomorrow you could be diagnosed with a fatal illness. Children growing up in "normal" circumstances don't think this way—they are going to live forever. But the well siblings of terminally ill children are introduced to the frailty of life early on. They no longer trust in the safety of their future because, as Phillip used to say, "Never quote me the odds."

The odds, in Brian's case, turned out to be fifty-fifty. He is a carrier of the recessive Friedreich's ataxia gene. He does not have FA, but he can pass the gene on to his children, so it will continue to lurk in the background of Brian's life. Luckily, his wife, Heather, has tested negative—she is not a carrier—so none of their children will have FA, but about half of them will still carry the gene on, for the next generation to worry about.

Brian is something of an old soul. He has lived with death lurking in the corner for most of his life and experienced the loss of his innocence too early. But he never completely gave up. Besides, his brother wouldn't have wanted him to.

Now Brian has to decide what to do with the life that has been given to him.

ᴡᴄᴀ ᴊᴍᴄᴍᴩᴦᴦᴦ ᴀᴍᴩᴦᴦᴩ

My Uncontrollable Wanderlust

Before I could walk, I had itchy feet. My parents love bragging to people that I flew twelve times before my first birthday. While still wearing a diaper, during a bomb scare at London's Heathrow airport, I was frisked! Convinced I wasn't packing, the authorities weren't satisfied until they emptied my travel bag and found only Duplo blocks. You know those commercials where babies make complicated online stock trades? Maybe, because of those, they thought I was capable of something precociously sinister. Seriously, did they expect to find explosives in my diaper?

Despite that early excitement (which, obviously, I don't remember) and despite the fact that the logistics are a pain in the ass, I love traveling. Ever wonder how someone like me, with absolutely no use of my legs, gets to and from an airplane seat? Yes, I'm that guy you get mad at (or jealous of) because I get to board first. "At this time we'll be boarding any passengers with special needs..." But, hey, give me a break! It's not like I don't need the help.

I also need a hell of a lot of patience and faith. Patience because I have to arrive at airports way before the typical passenger, then wait and wait and wait for assistance. Faith because I have to count on a bunch of airline pros to do their jobs. The reservationist has to get me an aisle seat. If I'm not flying with my dad (who can carry me to my seat), the gate attendants have to lift me onto a skinny little wheelchair and squeeze me down the center aisle (and, hopefully, not run over one of my dangling feet when, inevitably, one slips off the footrest). And who knows who has the job of ensuring that my own wheelchair is waiting for me at the arrival gate? Even though it has never been left behind, until my mom sticks her head out the door and tells me it's there, I stress over it.

Because I have Friedreich's ataxia, I have flown in more airplanes and been to more cities than most people my age (another small silver lining). When I was fourteen, my mom took me to my first National Ataxia Foundation annual conference. Since the conference moves around the country, I've been through multiple airports. It's surprising how different one experience can be from another, but most of the time the people I deal with are pretty great.

I don't mean for this to be a social commentary on airport security since that asshole Osama bin Laden attacked America, but—oh my gosh—do I look like a security threat! I guess so, because they always pat me down. Sometime with just a token touch, but sometimes they feel me up so thoroughly that I'm tempted to close my eyes and imagine that it's a hot blonde doing it, not some chunky TSA guy with a bad mustache.

One time, though, I did cause quite a security stir. On our way back from a rafting trip in Colorado, my mom and I were working our way through the security checkpoint inside the Grand Junction Regional Airport. We had gotten there in plenty of time, so we were unhurried and relaxed.

We entered the security area, expecting nothing but the usual nuisances. Then, when they examined my wheelchair, all hell broke loose. Alarms blared! My mom tried to rush to my aid but was held back. The TSA guy tried talking to me. But because the airport was crazy noisy and because of my not-so-easy-to-understand speech, we couldn't communicate. So, when they didn't find anything hazardous in my luggage, they agreed to let my mom onto the scene. She explained that my wheelchair and I were on our way home from a five-day Colorado River rafting trip.

"What's happening? Why the alarms? What has you so worried?" my mom wondered.

"Ma'am, we detected nitroglycerin on your son's wheelchair."

"Wait, what? That makes no sense," she said. "After we got out of the water on the last day, Phillip and his chair were disgustingly dirty, so I wheeled him into the hotel shower and scrubbed them both clean."

That was the clue the TSA guy was looking for. "Scrubbed them with what? Shampoo?"

"Yes."

"Ma'am, do you know what's in shampoo?"

"Soap?"

"Besides that."

"I don't know. Water? Perfume?"

"Ma'am, shampoo's ingredients include traces of glycerin."

Who knew?

Next, when they tried to test my chair again—just to make sure it wouldn't detonate in mid-flight—their washing-machine-sized chemical detector apparatus malfunctioned. We waited impatiently for at least an hour until they rolled in another, swabbed my chair, tested for residue, then, finally, relented and allowed us to proceed to our gate.

As soon as I got home, I couldn't wait to tell the story and spread the word to my ataxian friends, "Don't wash your wheelchair before going through security!"

Turns out I'm not the only one who has caused a nitro-glycerin scare. "Phil," more than one friend messaged me back, "before going through security, don't put on hand lotion!"

Guess what's in hand lotion?

Once I'm airborne there's not much for me to do. So, unless they're feeding me, I snooze. That's when I'm vulnerable. Like all FAers, I have a heightened startle reflex. When there's an unexpected noise, I jump—severely. The trouble is, air travel is inundated with sudden, out-of-nowhere sounds: Someone from the crew makes an announcement. The passenger behind me drops his tray. The baby beside me cries… When I'm startled, my knees jerk upward and I fall to my left or right.

My startle reflex has caused lots of drinks to spill onto my seat mates' laps. (Remember the time my meal ended up in the lap of the guy across the aisle?) So, after one too many of these embarrassing and awkward moments, my mom began bringing a portable seat belt on every trip. Prior to takeoff, she straps my chest to my seat back. It works, but it's one more hassle I wish we didn't have to deal with.

Nowadays, I often fly without my parents. But it wasn't easy to convince either one of them to let me do it. It took an invite from the Holohans to change their minds. Megan Holohan has FA. I met her at the National Friedreich's Ataxia conference in Costa

Mesa, California. I also connected well with Megan's parents, Sue and Dan, and with her brother and sister, Tyler and Sarah. Sarah is my age and we've become buddies, too.

The Holohans live in Chicago, and I desperately wanted to visit them there. I was about to turn sixteen, so, for my birthday, my parents agreed to let me fly alone to the Windy City. Back then, I was able to do much more for myself, but it still must have been hard for Mom and Dad to let me go.

It turned out to be the best present ever! The Holohans welcomed me into their home and were gracious and accommodating. They helped with everything I needed help with. They included me in their family gatherings and showed me Chicago. I even got to watch the Cubs play in Wrigley Field. Apparently, they liked having me, because they encouraged me to visit again. My birthday treks to Chicago became a tradition. I became an official grown-up when I turned eighteen at the Holohan casa. My visits there were special. They made me feel mature, independent, appreciated, and loved. My best memories are of the times when we'd build a campfire in the Holohan's backyard and sit around it and talk. Sarah, Megan, Tyler, and I would talk so long that, if my feet were too close to the fire, my shoe soles would melt.

As my conditioned worsened and I became more dependent, my Chicago trips ceased, but my times there will always be among my favorite memories. Not just because Chicago is a great city, but because of whom I was with when I was there. It's always about whom you're with. Great people equal great times.

My physical deterioration didn't decrease or deter my wanderlust. For example, during the summer of 2007, I added something to my life list: On New Year's Eve, December 31, 2007, I was going to watch the ball drop in Times Square. I didn't know how I was going to do it, but I was going to do it.

My mom offered to take me there. My dad did, too. But (no offense Mom and Dad) I didn't want them with me. Spending New Year's Eve in Times Square is a young person's thing. I wanted to be able to be wild and crazy without feeling like one of my parents would be hovering, watching my every move.

So I'd have to find myself a traveling companion/ aide. Since nobody came to mind, I decided to create a flier that said:

<u>Wanted: Personal Assistant—Traveling Companion</u>
Help Phillip Bennett achieve his dream. Spend New Year's Eve in Times Square, New York City!

The flier included photos of me looking my best. Truth is, I was hoping that a cute nursing or occupational therapy student would want the job. That didn't happen, but something almost as good did. I got to meet Eric Collins.

A friend of Eric's spotted one of my fliers hanging in San Jose State's child care center and told him about me. Eric had experience caring for and traveling with a man with another type of muscular dystrophy called Duchenne muscular dystrophy (DMD). That dude had needed even more intensive care than I would need, so Eric was more than qualified for the job.

Eric: *My friend Caroline was taking her daughter to the kindergarten program at San Jose State where she saw Phillip's flier. He needed an assistant to help take him to Times Square on New Year's Eve. "Eric," she said, "this might be something you'd be interested in."*

Before we left for New York, I drove up to Fremont so Valerie could train me on how to get Phillip up from bed and ready in the morning. We went out on a couple of little outings. We went to a concert in San Jose. Phil really liked that—flirting with all the girls. One time I took him down to Gilroy where I was helping out at a music festival. Phil seemed really happy; he said he thought this was the beginning of something cool.

And it was. What he said did come true. We did a lot of really amazing stuff. To get to know each other I would ride my bike to San Jose State University (SJSU) and meet him at the journalism building, then I'd push him over to the food court. I'd bring Buddy, my Chihuahua, and he would jump onto Phil's lap. Phil said Buddy was a chick magnet. We'd eat lunch, chill out a little bit, and then I'd push him to his next class.

Why New York in December? Phil told me how he would sit at home every year and watch the ball drop, and he "wanted to party with those guys." He wanted to do it on his own—in other words, no parents! When we landed at JFK, we were all, "Whooooo! We're here!" A minivan cab dropped us off right on 42nd Street, and we checked into our room. When we pushed back the curtain, we could see the Manhattan skyline. It was perfect! We had dinner at the Hard Rock Cafe, then we strolled around Times Square, stopping often to take pictures. We got to bed really late that night. Over the next couple of days, we saw the Rockettes at Radio City Music Hall, went to the observation deck on the Empire State Building, took in a comedy show, ate at B.B. King's, and watched a bunch of street performers. And of course we went to see the Statue of Liberty. We were inhaling the Big Apple, and the best was yet to come.

On New Year's Eve morning, Phillip insisted that we wake up early so we could get down to the curb early to get a good spot to watch the ball. We were there by about 1:00 p.m., so we ended up spending almost the whole day waiting for midnight.

If I could do it again I would have worn one of Phillip's spare condom catheters. For the first few hours while we were waiting, I could sneak away to a nearby pastry shop at the *corner to go to the bathroom. But after a few hours I couldn't get out of our "barrier pen." I was desperate to go, but trapped. I solved the problem by hiding behind Phillip and relieving myself into a cup.*

December 31, 2007, was icy cold. Phillip had on his electric socks, hand and foot warmers, ski pants, a down-filled jacket, two hats, and scarf and was still chilled. So was I.

Once the ball dropped, the crowd dispersed really quickly. I think it's because everybody was desperate to go to the bathroom. When the crowd thinned a bit, we lit up our stogies, and all these strangers (mostly ladies) stopped and had a picture taken with Phillip. He now has an album full of pictures of himself with a cigar in his mouth and a cute girl on either side.

No adventure would be complete without a snowstorm canceling the flight home, and our trip was no different. Just as we were preparing to spend the night at JFK airport, we got lucky and caught a late flight on Jet Blue to Oakland. We arrived home about 1:30 in the morning, exhausted but fulfilled.

Even though Eric's qualifications and experience put my parents' mind at ease, Mom wanted to be fully positive that our hotel room would be absolutely wheelchair accessible, complete with a roll-in shower. Fortunately, my friend Kim Perry worked near Times Square. Mom asked her if she would be willing to "inspect" the Hilton Times Square. She did, and even sent us a couple of pictures she took with her phone. The room met mom's standards, so we booked it.

The only catch was that once you book a hotel room for New Year's Eve on Times Square, you must pay for it immediately—and it's nonrefundable. As soon as I reserved the room, I was committed. The pressure was on for me to make sure the trip worked. Which was good. Remember what Goethe wrote about commitment?

Until one is committed, there is hesitancy, the chance to draw back—Concerning all acts of initiative (and creation), there is one elementary truth that ignorance of which kills countless ideas and splendid plans: that the moment one definitely commits oneself, then Providence moves too. All sorts of things occur to help one that would never otherwise have occurred. A whole stream of events issues from the decision, raising in one's favor all manner of unforeseen incidents and meetings and material assistance, which no man could have dreamed would have come his way. Whatever you can do, or dream you can do, begin it. Boldness has genius, power, and magic in it. Begin it now.

Note: There is some question as to whether or not Goethe wrote this. But who cares? No matter who wrote it, it's fricken awesome!

We spent a full week in NYC. And when I say full, I mean full. Prior to the New Year's Eve festivities, we hit Radio City Music Hall and checked out the Rockettes (thumbs up!), went to the top of the Empire State Building, ferried over to the Statue of Liberty, did a city tour, ate at the Hard Rock Cafe, and met with a bunch of my East Coast friends. Eric was surprised by how many people I knew in New York. I was kind of surprised myself.

The only negative was the weather. It was cold as hell that week. I know it's always cold there at that time of year, but even the native New Yorkers told us it was abnormally frigid. But I didn't care. I was there, bundled up and among the throng of humanity that is Times Square on New Year's Eve. The organization was impressive. We were advised to get there early (great advice, except that by midnight my face felt frostbitten) and find a place in a special area barricaded off for people in wheelchairs. Unfortunately, this was not near the stage, so no one saw me on TV, but it was still a great place to be. Even though I was immersed in a pack of delirious party people, I could see everything clearly. When the ball dropped, and AD 2008 dawned, Eric and I lit up our stogies.

It must have been hard for mom to hear about how fun and successful and great my trip was. Even though I'm sure she was happy for me, I wondered if she was hurt by me wanting to go to New York—to travel anywhere—without her...

Mom: *I was Phillip's enthusiastic advocate when it came to his wanderlust. When he was fifteen and begging to go to Chicago to visit the Holohans, I was all for it. We had met them and really wanted him to have the experience of traveling alone. His dad was not so ready to let him go. But when Tim asked me what Phillip would like for his sixteenth birthday, I told him, "If you want to give him what he wants more than anything else, let him go to Chicago." And he did.*

The first of Phillip's solo flights was before the additional security imposed by the post-9/11 world. His Dad and I would take him all the way to the gate, and even (with some cajoling of the airport staff) help them get Phillip settled into his seat on the plane, and batten down his wheelchair for transport in the hold of the plane. Before heading back home, we would wait in the boarding lounge until the plane taxied and took off. When he returned home, we would be waiting to help them get him off the plane.

By the time he flew to New York, things were different. Not only were we in a whole new world of security, Phillip's physical abilities had deteriorated significantly. He could no longer move his manual wheelchair himself, and he needed help with showering, dressing, eating—everything. Traveling "alone," Phillip would be very vulnerable.

I was able to support this trip because I had confidence in his aide's ability to take care of Phillip's needs. Eric Collins had traveled with a quadriplegic man with Duchenne muscular dystrophy, so I felt I could rely on him. I could also be sure that the hotel room was truly wheelchair accessible. Phillip's friend, Kim Perry, was able to visit the Hilton Times Square, check out the accessible room and take pictures, all of which helped allay my fears.

As memorable as these trips were, though, they were just longer, farther, and more complicated versions of the act of faith that took place every morning when Paratransit (hopefully) picked Phillip up and took him off to San Jose State University. He was dependent and vulnerable every time. What if Paratransit was late? What if it was pouring rain? What if Phillip misjudged a ramp and tipped his wheelchair

over sideways (with him in it) ending up in the shrubbery?
(This happened more than once.) What if he wasn't able to
get from his last class to his pickup point in time? Phillip and
I both had faith that each day would work out somehow. We
both trusted that he would, when needed, be able to rely on
help from someone, and his experience served to strengthen
that trust.

I had a conversation with the father of a young woman
with ataxia, and he told me that he does not like her to take
public transportation. She can still walk, although she falls,
and he is afraid she will fall without him around to help
her up. I tried to help him understand that it won't be a bad
thing for her to fall without him there. A total stranger will be
moved to help her, and they will both be enriched by the expe-
rience. I had learned this myself, so I tried to explain to him
that he is actually depriving her of this experience if he shelters
her. He would be depriving her of the opportunity to see the
goodness of people around her and discover that she can trust
and depend on others.

I suspect that things happened that I don't know any-
thing about, and that I would be horrified if I did know!
But it doesn't matter. What does matter is that Phillip forged
ahead, without trepidation, often into completely uncharted
territory for him, strengthened by his many experiences with
the kindness and generosity of complete strangers.

I don't want to come off as all preachy here, but
here's the truth: There are ways to make things hap-

pen. You just have to find those ways. I mean, it didn't make much sense for a guy with Friedreich's ataxia to dream of celebrating New Year's Eve with a million people on a freezing winter evening in Times Square. Making it happen was an incredible ordeal. But it happened. It happened because I wanted it badly, committed to it fully, and got a lot of people to help me. If you want something that, at first, doesn't seem sensible or even possible, keep those three things in mind: Want it badly, commit to it fully, and ask for help.

Investment banker and former Coca-Cola president Donald Keough said, "What separates those who achieve from those who do not is in direct proportion to one's ability to ask for help." I'd be nowhere and, literally, go nowhere, if I was ashamed to ask for help.

In this way, are you any different from me?

ᒑ ᒉᒧᒬᒉ ᒑᒃᒧ

A D e g r e e   A b o v e

Exchanging one last laugh with his journalism professor, Dr. Richard Craig, at Phillip's graduation from San Jose State University.

From Ho-Ho-Kus-Cogitator – March 2011
Reprinted with permission

Harvey Gotliffe, PhD
Professor of Journalism and Mass Communication
San Jose State University

After teaching writing courses for more than twenty-five years at far too many universities, I am unable to accurately count the number of students who have sat in my classes. As for specific students, professors tend to remember those who were at the extreme ends of the spectrum—the students who were unadulterated pains, and those who made teaching worthwhile.

In the latter category I would easily place Phillip Bennett; the most valiant student I have ever known. Phillip was witty, articulate, a brilliant thinker, at times harmlessly mischievous, and was one of the most intelligent and articulate of my student writers.

If you were a professor or another student, you were fortunate enough to learn from him if you took the time to learn about him. He stood out from the moment you first met him and yet he was always sitting down.

Phillip had many enviable traits within the classroom, and when he set himself loose from its limiting confines, he soared while skydiving and hang gliding, roared attempting waterskiing, white-water rafting, and rappelling down Mount Diablo. He always wanted to try something new and different and to celebrate New Year's 2008 he decided to go to New York and smoke a stogie. He put a notice on the university bulle-

tin board, and with some newfound companions, lit up and "became part of the human marmalade in Times Square."

He Defined Who He Was

Almost everything Phillip attempted from the age of thirteen on, he did in his wheelchair, but he never let the wheelchair define who he was or what he was capable of doing. Phillip was blessed with a contagious but realistic positive attitude, yet from the age of ten on he was cursed with the debilitating Friedreich's ataxia disease. It is a rare disorder that picks off nerve cells, and Phillip was optimistic after he learned that some with the disease had lived into their thirties and forties.

The Write Stuff

Phillip came to San Jose State University in 2003 and became a student of mine in the School of Journalism in 2007. His mother, Valerie, brought him to the first class session and explained that his heart began failing the previous fall, and wrote in an e-mail, "He is very aware that his time is limited." She added, "Phillip loves to write. It's about the last remaining thing he can do."

Helping Others

In my writing classes, in groups of three, students would edit each other's assignments before they would be rewritten and turned in to me. Phillip was so astute and insightful in his evaluations and so profoundly helpful in his editing, others clamored to be in his group.

Once when I looked at his gnarled and crooked fingers, I asked him how he managed to type up his brilliant editing evaluations and his own beautifully written assignments, thinking he was getting some sort of voice-recognition software. He said that he types very slowly using just one finger and hitting one key at a time. Whenever I had a student complain about the difficulties of typing a paper, I quietly told him Phillip's story.

My writing classes usually held less than twenty students and I wanted them to know one another. During the semester, I had every student briefly interview all of the other students in the class. At the end of the semester, the final examination consisted of each student turning in a paragraph about all of the other students in the class.

Who Does He Think He Is?

Phillip followed the instructions and wrote a mini-profile of all of the other students in his own inimitable way, and then he decided to describe himself and do so in the third person. "He was originally majoring in psychology, but decided to shift his focus to writing when he observed that girls in the Journalism Department were cuter." Phillip's mischievous side came forth when he confessed to having one of his four tattoos put on in the kitchen while his mom's Bible study group was meeting in the next room. He also wrote, "His bondage to a wheelchair has not held him back." But his wheelchair maneuverability caused him consternation and aggravation more than once.

Running Wild

Phillip earned a small gash in his forehead after he ended up in the shrubbery while traversing uncontrollably down a ramp at too great a speed. In a convoluted incident, he inadvertently backed his wheelchair into a partially blind coed who reported the incident to the university police. Phillip and his mother sorted the matter out at the police building and it caused him to miss one of my class sessions. He sent me an apologetic e-mail and when he wrote an article in Access, *the university's student magazine, he described the woman's reaction. "Of all of the toes I have run over, the only person to react with anger was another disabled person. I realized just by looking at her that she was exactly what I could be if I was not so positive about life."*

He Did What He Could

Phillip's positive energy abounded, and he took charge of whatever time he had left when he decided to try and raise money for a cure, and if one occurred, he knew it would be after his life was over. He avowed, "It is my disability, my burden, my life and I will fight for it." Fight he did and through Herculean efforts, his fund raising efforts raised more than $200,000.

It's My Party

When Phillip earned a Bachelor of Science degree in spring 2008, I joined his many friends, relatives, and his fellow church members who crowded the hall at his joyous graduation party. It was also a celebration of Phillip Bennett's extremely worthwhile life, and he enjoyed the party immensely. Fate is in and out of our hands, and I was dazed by the incongruity of watching Phillip ensconced in his wheelchair, kibitzing as he always did with his robust, healthy, six-two, twenty-one-year-old athletic "little brother," Brian.

It's My Story

After graduation, Phillip sent me an e-mail asking me how to go about writing and publishing the story of his life. I told him of the many ways to go and wrote, "Your life story is one of great importance, and I keep your Access article close by as my own inspiration." Phillip's autobiography was two-thirds completed when I received an e-mail from Phillip's mother that began with "I have very sad news. Phillip passed away on March 2. We are trying to figure out how to get through each day without him." His mother and a newspaper columnist are working on finishing his book for him. He would have been twenty-seven on July 8, and he lived a full, yet too short of a life. The tattoo inked as a band around his left bicep emphasizes the message he lived his life by, "All you have to decide is what to do with the time that is given to you." It's something perhaps more of us should ink into our minds.

Phillip's Stepdad, Tom: *He and I had the best one-on-one time together when he was attending San Jose State University and I was working at San Jose City Hall. We met on Wednesdays for lunch. We always went to Subway, mainly because that was the type of food he could hold in his hand and eat unassisted.*

He would always get the Italian BMT Sub with extra meat, extra cheese, and no veggies. I said to him, "Boy, if you ate these every day, it would kill you." He just laughed and said, "But they're soooo good." Then we would eat outside at the intersection of two main walks where the greatest number of girls would go by. Once in a while someone would recognize him and would come over and say, "How you doing, Phil?" That made Phillip's day.

þA bɨ̃ỡ qApͥρ́ỹ
The Final Chapter

Wednesday, February 23, 2011—Phillip's Facebook status:

...sick as a dog. Can barely breathe, barely speak, and I've been miserable since I woke up Monday morning. Waiting for the doctor to call back...

Mom: *Phillip had contracted a nasty winter cold. He visited the doctor and was given antibiotic eyedrops and a prescription for oral antibiotics. On Monday, February 28, after he became progressively worse, we returned to the doctor for a chest x-ray. No pneumonia was detected.*

Phillip spent Tuesday in bed, with his wonderful, loyal aide, Jamie, bringing him lots of fluids. He was extraordinarily thirsty. When I returned home from work that afternoon, I was concerned about his coloring. His skin tone was gray, and his lips were pallid. I checked his blood pressure but couldn't get a reading. Phillip hadn't eaten all day, so I warmed some homemade turkey soup and managed to spoon nearly two bowls of it into him. As sick as he was, he still loved to eat!

I tucked him into bed. Again, I tried to take his blood pressure. Again I couldn't get a reading. Concerned, I phoned our friend and neighbor, Mary Nolan. Mary is a nurse, and I needed to ask her if she thought I should take him to the emergency room. Mary was terrific. She got Phillip to laugh (for the very last time in his life) and found a way to get some color back into his lips. But it rapidly faded. She couldn't get a blood pressure reading either, so she said yes: I should get him to the hospital.

It was 8:30 p.m. I got Phillip dressed, back into his wheelchair, into the van, and drove him the two and a half miles from our house to the emergency room. As soon as we parked, the ER staff leaped into action. It was like a scene from one of those fictional hospital dramas. Only in this case, it was devastatingly real.

While I was still checking him in, Phillip was whisked away. In the short time it took me to get him registered, nurses had him out of his wheelchair, onto a hospital bed, and were prepping him for an IV. I introduced myself to the ER doctor and began filling her in on Phillip's condition, symptoms, and complications. I expressed my unease about the IV fluids, as I had on several previous occasions when Phillip had been hospitalized. Excessive fluids could overload his fragile heart. There is a history of this causing the death of Friedreich's ataxians. In each previous case, the medical staff was appreciative of the warning and changed their treatment accordingly. This time, however, was different. The doctor looked me in the eye, fully acknowledging my distress, and said, "Right now we're trying to save his life. If we're successful, we'll worry about the damage we do to his heart later."

Thus, while they desperately tried to save Phillip's life, I experienced the worst moments of mine. The doctor explained that Phillip was in septic shock. According to the National Institutes of Health, septic shock is "a serious condition that occurs when an overwhelming infection leads to life-threatening low blood pressure." The trauma team (which kept expanding) pushed IV fluids (literally squeezing bags of liquids) into Phillip, urgently attempting to raise his blood volume and pressure. They tried four lines and four bags, but there was no improvement. They asked me to step behind the curtain while they inserted a cardiac catheter in through his neck to monitor his heart. I complied, but now I wish I hadn't. After all I had been through with Phillip in hospitals, there was nothing I hadn't already seen. Lurking behind the curtain, I heard Phillip call for me. Immediately, I rushed back to him.

His blood pressure was dangerously low, and his brain was being deprived of oxygen. A doctor asked for my permission to ventilate him. I consented. This was a critical step—the first one toward life support. But there'd be no point in saving his life if his brain wasn't receiving oxygen.

The ventilation complete, Phillip was now unable to speak. He had spoken his last words, only it wasn't clear what they were. Because he was sinking into an oxygen-deprivation mental fog, he couldn't speak clearly. I wish I had spent a private moment with him before they ventilated him—that way I could have focused on what he was saying. But at the time, we were all fixated on trying to save his life. The atmosphere was frantic. Doctors raced to turn the tide of the falling blood pressure that would deprive not just his brain, but all his organs of oxygen until, eventually, they would fail. So Phillip's last words will forever be a mystery. It's one more huge regret to add to my pile.

Phillip's father arrived with his wife. He and I were taken aside to answer the excruciatingly tough questions and go over the frustratingly necessary paperwork. By the time we got back to the emergency room, a swarm of doctors, nurses, and machines were hovered around Phillip in a frantic attempt to save his life. Tim and Ruth and Tom and I huddled together on the side, watching the dreadful drama unfold.

Five hours after he entered the emergency room, Phillip's heart stopped beating. The team's intensity level ratcheted up to the extreme. Despite the terrifying desperation, I asked if I could move to a spot close to Phillip's head. I couldn't stand being unable to touch him, unable to let him know that I was still there. The nurses let me wind my way through an obstacle course of cables and medical contraptions so I could stand next to him. Living a nightmare, I watched someone wheel over an echocardiogram machine. Over the years, I've seen dozens of Phillip's echocardiograms. Each time, I was amazed at how valiantly his heart beat, never ever able to rest. But this time was different. This time his heart was still.

I don't know when he lost consciousness. The ventilator kept his chest rising and falling, each breath artificial. I don't know if he was aware that I had made my way to his side. I don't know if he felt me kissing his forehead. I don't know if he knew I was with him, clinging to him. The uncertainty haunts me to this day. It will forever haunt me.

Machines were switched off and carted away. The subdued staff withdrew. Eventually, it was just Phillip and I alone in the room. Inconsolably sobbing, I kissed every inch of his body, that poor, frail body that had fought so hard for so long against the ravages of Friedreich's ataxia. That intrepid body covered with bruises, scrapes, scratches, and scars from the abuse that a life of spasms, falls, accidents, and surgeries had wreaked upon it.

I kissed each wound. I wrapped my arms around his brave body. A body that had jumped from airplanes, but never had the arms of a lover around it. I kissed the lips that had so often formed the smile that lit up so many lives, but had never been kissed by a girlfriend. Very slowly, I said good-bye to the one human being with whom I was more connected than any other. We had been joined at the hip, and I felt like I had been torn in two. For seventeen years we had fought Friedreich's ataxia together, but as relentlessly as we fought, it was a battle we could not win. For the rest of my life, I will never again feel completely whole.

Tribute

The fact that Phillip James Bennett was loved by those who knew him (and by many of those who had only a brief encounter with him) is evidenced by what happened after he passed. Although those cursed with Friedreich's ataxia don't usually live a long life, those who knew Phillip were convinced he would live much longer than he did. When you were with him, you felt like he'd live forever.

In a very practical way, he will. Phillip's warm, strong, positive spirit was injected into the hearts of so many others that it initiated an inexorable ripple that continues to expand and impact.

Social media was a vital part of Phillip's life. It was especially important during his early adult years. No longer in school, unemployed, confined to his wheelchair, sometimes feeling trapped in his bedroom, the Internet was his window to the world. Facebook was vital to his social welfare. It was his way of communicating with friends, far and near.

When Phillip Bennett died, his Facebook page did not disappear. It's a strange, new issue. What should you do with people's online content after their death? Not, what *can* you do? What *should* you do?

As with most aspects of the Internet, it depends on how it's used. The way Phillip's Facebook page has been and continues to be used should be a model for what *to* do. Starting with the poignant "About" section in which he describes himself as an *"independent author, at home, working on his autobiography"* to the heart-wrenching yet beautifully and lovingly written good-byes, to the birthday messages that continue to be posted each year on July 8, Phil's Facebook page is a classy, tasteful tribute to the boy and man who deeply affected way more people than he knew he had.

ｂｙᴅ ｐㅅᴏᴏᴘ'ᴌ ｂᴞｊᴘᵍ ｐᴮᴊ

A sampling of some of the hundreds of messages written to Phillip since his final post.

Phil Bennett (final FB post)

is sick as a dog. Can barely breathe, barely speak, and I've been miserable since I woke up Monday morning. Waiting for the doctor to call back...

Marco Mastroprimiano

Get well soon. FA + sick = nobody quite understands how bad we feel.

Phil Bennett

My Mom is writing this for me to let you all know that I fought my last battle with Friedreich's ataxia last night. I finally got my honorable discharge papers and was able to go home, "Mission Accomplished." Mom is devastated.

Marylee Sheffer

I think that you did more than accomplish your mission, Phil. I think you changed the world. Thanks for being part of my life! Love you!

Sue Knight Kittel

Raft in Peace...

Mimi Sheffer

Phillip Bennett, you dirty rotten scoundrel, we had plans for spring break, and you bailed! What the hell, Man, that beer isn't gonna drink itself. I knew eventually you'd take off (and probably without a goodbye), but knowing it really, really didn't make it any easier. I'm sorry I didn't make it back in time. It's gonna be a long road without you.

Renee Firato

Phil you always were such an inspiration to me. Your smile and kind heart always made my day. You're a testament of strength, faith and hope. I am so sad to hear about your passing but it helps ease the pain knowing you are healed and no longer in pain. You did beat your battle with Friedreich's ataxia—and I know you are running around in heaven making everyone laugh. I know you're an Angel now so you are always with us. You are missed greatly and I will never forget your smile. Thank you for the strength you inspired in me, the caring friend you always were and the everlasting impression you have made in my life. Your family was blessed with an Angel—you Phil.

Felice Barash

Phil, I feel honored to be able to say that you were my friend. I am so sad that you are gone and will miss you more than words explain. I am so sorry and regret that we did not get the opportunity to see each other this year. When I think of you, I think of the strength that you had despite the times that you were feeling down. You made the most of life and accomplished so much in your near 27 years. I am so glad that I was able to share some shining, fun, happy moments with you from winter ball to sky diving, to fund-raising events. I look forward to reading your book and will always have very fond memories of you and with you. May you rest in peace. - love, Felice.

Sophia Sieber-Davis

Be in Peace Phil...who knows if you're resting... maybe you're continuing fun adventures, seeing all the places we talked about in the travel magazine with our hot chocolate! I remember all the amazing stories you had, and I can't believe you just visited me in my sick bed. I'm sorry I didn't get to visit you. Thank you for your unwavering smile and as Kyle said, strengthening our resolve for a cure.

Ashley Hartigan

Phil Bennett(: It was an honor knowing you. Even though at first I thought you were crazy, because you were mumbling and I had absolutely no idea what you were saying. You inspire me. And I will always be thankful for that. I love you, and you will be missed! Have fun with the ladies up there!

Brent Pennelly

I always thought it was unfair that someone with as much energy and happiness as you should be born with FA. For most people, it would hold them back, yet you truly lived larger than life—how did you do that? Turn what most would call a disability into a distant afterthought? You're an inspiration to more people than you know. May you rest in peace.

Jamie Plourde

Meeting you is something I'm proud of. I want to finish what you started. Thanks for all of the laughs, Sweetie. I'll see you again one day. No mean jokes with Aaron Kittel! At least not on me;) Love you.

Mimi Sheffer

From January until the day I heard you'd died, I was planning on how to talk you into coming back to camp (AGAIN). Just for a few hours. Enough to remind you of how much everyone loves you there.

So I could feel like my whole family was back together again. The first time I truly *understood* you were going to die young was at camp. It was over ten years ago (we were probably around 14 or 15), and it was during that last Saturday service where we all stand around and cry and hug. I sat on a bench with Alison, and we cried and tried to figure out why we weren't as invincible as we felt. I didn't remember any of this until we sat down this past Saturday and Doug started talking. I cried through the entire service, until my eyes were burning and my sweater was soaked through and I couldn't sing or look anywhere other than at my chipped nail polish because it was too hard to look anyone in the eye. I miss you, man.

Brian Leitner

It was an honor. Your strength and will, humor and charisma outshined all that put you to rest. May peace be with you and your family.

Travis Silva

Phil, your courage and strength touched me and so many others. I wish you had had more time to teach us all how to live. Rest well.

Yusef Carrillo

I cannot make sangria without you. I will miss you, my cousin and friend.

Giancarlo Moats

Sharing that trek up the hill to MSJ every morning was a pleasure. Watching you humble the rest of us throwers at track practice with your determination was an honor. This world will be a little darker without you, but your personal example will continue on as something for all of us to aspire to. I consider myself lucky to have known you, and I was truly blessed to have been your friend.

Amanda Kahn

What a huge loss to the world. Thank you for your indomitable spirit, nonchalant bravery, and sense of humor. Between the rock climbing, connections with people, fund-raising, writing a book, skydiving, and all of the other activities you did, you lived more in 27 years than many people do in 70. It was always so great to go out and joke around during track practice. My sympathy goes out to all of your family and many friends.

Erika Brown

What a huge loss for the world, Phil. Everyone you ever met, you touched their lives in a positive way. You never let anything hold you back despite any physical hardships. You had an inspiring spirit, one that inspired others to want to try to help people...You reminded me why I became a nurse in the first place, and made others want to have that "I am invincible, nothing can stop me!!" spirit, too...You will be missed, but never forgotten...My thoughts and prayers are with you and your family.

Kim Alves

Phil, some of us were lucky enough to have you grace our lives. I know I am one of them and am very grateful that you were in my life. I miss you and I know a lot of other people do also. Thank you for being you.

Kim Perry

Oh Phil, not sure I have the right words here—but you had more courage than just about anyone I know. You have always been an inspiration to me—you did so much, you touched so many, you had the remarkable ability to bulldoze through just about any "challenge" that crossed your path. I'm so sorry I didn't get to church this Christmas; it would have been wonderful to see you one last time. Hugs to your family.

Shelby Connich

You were an inspiration to every person you came into contact with the way you were able to attack life with everything it threw at you and make the most of it. You will be truly missed.

James Squires

Sending out much love to you and your family, Phil. I hate so to see you go, but your body was a source of so much trouble. I take comfort in knowing you are now free of it and can enjoy the next phase in freedom. Thanks for all the times we had.

Brandon Sonn

You were a great example of someone who maintained a positive attitude and continued to persevere despite adversity and the constant challenges life throws at all of us. You are truly an inspiration and lived to an extent we should all strive to achieve. I'm still in shock at your passing and you will be greatly missed. I'm so very glad to have known you and to have been a part of your life, and I was lucky to have had you in mine. Rest in peace my good friend.

Helium Magazine

Today honors the life of Phil Bennett. A wickedly talented writer with an infectious smile and an insatiable need to skydive. Phil inspired those around him with his unwavering bravery. His spirit lives on through those whose lives he touched, and his legacy in journalism is eternal. Our thoughts and prayers go out to his family. May he forever rest in peace.

Arturo Navarro

Phil, you are a testament to the fact that anything is possible and that nothing should hold us back from our dreams. I'm very grateful for the times we got to hang out at camp. You definitely kept things interesting! You will be missed, but also remembered. Keep it Philthy!

Ashley Hartigan

Phil, you are the strongest, toughest, most dedicated, full of life, inspirational man I know. I thought you were crazy, but now I know that you are crazy. Everything you face, your head is held high with that unforgettable smile (: You have made me who I am. I don't know who I'd be if I hadn't met you. You will always be in my thoughts and prayers. I could never forget you, my friend. That mumbling from behind is my crazy buddy and will always hold a special place in my heart. Thank you for everything that you have done in this world. Bring your high spirits on with you and I'll meet up with you some day. Everyone you met, you inspired. I love you Phil! (:

Love forever and always, Ashley Irene Hartigan — One of many you inspired

Brice Yett

Phil...today we all said goodbye and celebrated your amazingly full life. There were lots of tears shed and many laughs as we remember the man you were: strong, sweet, dedicated, brave, insanely smart, funny, charismatic, charming, a wonderful friend...the list goes on because words can't describe just how special you are! God has a bigger plan for you now as you go home to him. May you rest in peace and be free to fly. I know you have your wings...Watch over us and give us the strength to live our lives every day as you lived yours — making each second count and being thankful for what we have been given. You will always be in my thoughts and in my heart...I am so blessed to have known you. Through the tears I smile because I know you would want us to smile. We will never forget you...

Eric Collins

"You should leave this world better than you found it." Phil really lived that. Going to his memorial service and going to the ataxia conference afterwards woke me up and motivated me to try to make a difference. Looking back on what Phillip said on our way back from our first outing together, he was right; it was an amazing journey, and it's not over yet. The project isn't over—even finishing this book isn't the end of the journey, as long as the influence of Phillip's life is being felt in the world.

ᴘᴧᴑ ᴄᴊᴘᴄ ᴘᴧ ᴑᴇᴘ ᴀᴣᴘ

The Last Word
A Final Essay
by Phillip Bennett

Spring 2008
San Jose State University
Excerpted from *Access* Magazine
"Making the Decision"

I wanted to do what everybody who is normal does, and I wanted to be as normal as I could be. I keep going because I am surrounded by caring, accepting, accommodating individuals who go out of their way to support me and treat me like a real person.

I was unfortunate enough to physically run into a blind student on campus. Her reaction shocked me. She was so livid she called the University Police Department. The officer who responded told me he could not even repeat what she said about me. Of all the toes I have run over in all the years I've been wheeling, the only person to react with anger was another disabled person. I realized just by looking at her that she was exactly what I could be if I was not so positive about life.

I have learned as I have journeyed through life in this wheelchair that most people are really wonderful. They go out of their way to help me get through my day. They push me up a ramp here, open a door there, take notes in class for me, or pick me up from the dirt under the shrubbery when I have fallen. The vast majority of people want to help; they just need to be asked. People stepped forward to donate time, money, and services to our annual fund-raiser because I asked them and thanked them. It may seem unfathomable for a $200,000 charitable campaign to have been hatched in the back seat of a minivan by an overly ambitious teenager on a road trip, but as hard as it is to believe, it can happen. It did for me.

A mere young adult in a wheelchair achieved all this, so imagine the possibilities that are open to you. My goal is not to change the world single-handedly, but to motivate and inspire others to help me change it. My point for you is that any dream, no matter how far-fetched it may seem, is attainable. If a once-reserved kid in a wheelchair was able to overcome his own obstacles and pursue a dream that wielded so much, then I challenge you to go out into the world and make it better.

I may not have much time left, but I can still leave a lasting impression on the world through my actions. **This is what I have chosen to do with the time that is given to me.**

(To see more pictures of what Phillip chose to do with the time that was given to him, please visit www. livingthedecision.com.)

Afterword – Lessons from Phil

Five lessons Phil would want you to learn

1. Find a way – Not bragging, but if I could do some of the things I did, surely you can overcome your obstacles

2. Get help – I couldn't have done much of anything without help. Don't be afraid to ask for it. Most people are much more helpful than you think.

3. Don't whine. Everybody's life is hard, but yours is probably better than most. Make the most of what you do have, and stop complaining about what you don't have!

4. Contribute to the world. Cheer someone up. Laugh. Have fun. Find a cause. Raise money for it or help out in some other way. May I suggest FARA (Friedreich's Ataxia Research Alliance)?

5. All of our lives are finite. Stop living like you have forever. French philosopher and activist, Simone de Beauvoir said, "If all it does is maintain itself, then living is only not dying." Don't just maintain yourself. Plan for the future, but don't forget to sometimes live like you don't have one.

Made in the USA
Middletown, DE
29 July 2017